DINING IN WITH THE GREAT CHEFS OF
SEATTLE
C·O·O·K·B·O·O·K

DINING IN WITH THE GREAT CHEFS OF SEATTLE

C·O·O·K·B·O·O·K

A Collection of Gourmet Recipes for Complete Meals
from the Seattle Area's Finest Restaurants

ELAINE LOTZKAR, REBECCA BETHEL,
KAREN GREGORAKIS MALODY

Foreword by
Elliott Wolf

Peanut Butter Publishing
Seattle, Washington

Cover Photography: Chris Conrad
Styling & Design: Charmaine Eades
Photographer's and Stylist's Assistant: Anne White
Cover Design: Suzy Whittaker
Production: Susan Irwin
Typesetting: Angus McGill, Julie Lloyd

CONTENTS

ACKNOWLEDGEMENTS

We would like to thank Mel Carlson, Bob Valentine, Robert Frayn, Joe Calabro and Roy Johnson at Valco Graphics for all of their assistance, without which this book would not have been possible.

FOREWORD

We at Peanut Butter Publishing are proud to present this new volume of *Dining In–Seattle*. It is more than just a traditional cookbook, it is a compilation of success stories. It represents the achievements of many Seattle restaurateurs who, aided by the hard work and dedication to excellence of numerous farmers, fishermen and chefs, have continued to provide the finest dining experiences available.

Our goal has been to bring you, the reader and gourmet, delicious and exciting recipes from these most interesting and successful restaurants. It has been the goal of these 25 restaurants to maintain the highest standards in food preparation, presentation and attention to detail that make dining out in Seattle the experience it is.

We hope you will agree that these goals have been met and we at Peanut Butter Publishing are on to the future. The publication of this compilation of *Dining In* Volumes II and III marks the end of one phase of our publishing tradition and the beginning of a new and exciting one.

Our new series of publications, the *Series of Distinctive Dining* and *The Epicures* will focus on bringing you the best dining experience available either in or outside of the home. This *Series of Distinctive Dining* will highlight complete menus and recipes of the finest restaurants in 40 major metropolitan areas while *The Epicures* are menu guides to the best and most innovative restaurants in 21 major areas. There will also be a *National Epicure* featuring the finest restaurants across the country. The remarkable success of the past *Dining In's* and *Epicures* have given us the impetus to move on to this next phase. Both the *Dining In* and *Epicure* series' have sold over a million copies nationwide and continue to bring requests from all facets of the population and sales around the world.

The future is bright at Peanut Butter Publishing and it is only fitting that it begin with this book on Seattle, an area we consider to be of unlimited culinary possibilities. We feel certain that there is no place in the country that can offer the raw materials for fine cooking that we can find in our spectacular surroundings.

With book in hand, the irresistible aromas and tastes of the 25 best restaurants in Seattle, the very essence of northwestern cuisine, are in your possession. We sincerely hope that you enjoy preparing the recipes as much as we and the restaurants have enjoyed bringing them to you.

ADRIATICA
CUCINA MEDITERRANEA

Dinner for Four

Asparagus or Leeks in Prosciutto with Herb Mayonnaise

John's Mostaccioli

Greek Potatoes

Costarelle

Vegetables Provençale

Dates and Walnuts in Fillo

Wine:

With Asparagus and Mostaccioli—Grgich Hill Fumé Blanc, 1980

With Costarelle—Taurasi, 1973 or Beaujolais, Morgon, 1978

Connie and Him Malevetsis, Owners

Nancy Flume, Executive Chef

ADRIATICA

The Adriatica is addictive: once there, you never want to leave; once gone, you want to go back. Much of this has to do with the familial sense about the place—genuinely warm greetings offered by owners Connie and Jim Malevetsis and the intimate, homelike setting the two have created at the restaurant. All this in combination with superb, authentically prepared Mediterranean-style cuisine makes for one of the most successful and popular restaurants in Seattle.

Located in a lovely, old house close to the downtown area, the Adriatica is elegantly decorated with finely crafted woodwork. Downstairs there are four unique rooms, and the newly constructed upstairs features an outdoor deck, breathtaking views of Lake Union and Lake Washington, and a full bar complete with appetizers.

The menu epitomizes the simple, straightforward concepts on which the restaurant was based over six years ago. Connie and executive chef Nancy Flume still get together every Monday morning to plan the weekly specials, among which two fresh and local seafood dishes, two new desserts, and various selections of pasta are constants. The regular fare includes the ever-popular *raznijici*—a Yugoslavian marinated, grilled lamb—a delicious fresh linguini with asparagus prosciutto and Parmesan cheese, and a baked garlic dish served on a crouton with French montrachet cheese. The calamari fritti and souvlaki appetizers of the Adriatica are by now Seattle legends.

Innovative ideas are always being sought at the Adriatica. The owners' recent voyage and research in Italy and southern France are already providing even more delightful possibilities. The mixed grill entrée, consisting of two fresh lamb chops marinated in red wine and olive oil and served with homemade Italian sausage and spicy polenta, is their latest. Accompanied with an individually prepared chocolate soufflé and an extensive wine list, this feast assures a supreme dining experience for which the Adriatica has become renowned.

1107 Dexter North

ASPARAGUS OR LEEKS IN PROSCIUTTO

Leeks and asparagus are equally delicious in this simple salad, depending on which is in season or most readily available. Experiment with other vegetables, too—few would be ill-suited to this straightforward presentation.

1 to 1½ pounds fresh asparagus (depending on size)	HERB MAYONNAISE
¼ pound high-quality prosciutto, thinly sliced	Lemon slices (optional)

1. Trim off the thicker outer skin of the asparagus. Cut the stalks into even lengths. Tie together with kitchen string or wrap a band of aluminum foil around the bundle. Set the bundle, trimmed ends down, in a deep pot containing 1 inch of boiling salted water, to insure that the delicate tips are only steamed—not immersed—in water. Steam in this manner only until the asparagus turns bright green and is still quite crunchy.

2. Remove from the water, untie, and plunge into cold water to stop the cooking process and seal in the color and flavor. Dry thoroughly on a clean towel or paper towels.

3. Count the prosciutto slices. If the number will not make four equal portions, set aside any extra slices for other use. Spread the prosciutto slices with some of the Herb Mayonnaise. Place an equal portion of asparagus on each slice and roll into a bundle.

4. Place the bundles, evenly divided, among four salad plates. Spoon a dollop of Herb Mayonnaise atop each bundle, passing the remaining mayonnaise at the table should guests desire more sauce. Garnish with lemon slices, if desired.

Note: If using leeks, select young, tender stalks and cut off the greens at the point where they begin to be tough. Bring 2 to 3 quarts water to a boil in a pot; just before adding the whole leeks, add 1 tablespoon baking soda to the water (to help retain the green and tenderize the leeks). Boil until tender. Remove from water, plunge into cold water to stop the cooking process, dry thoroughly, and cut into halves or quarters lengthwise, depending on how large the leeks are. Proceed as with the asparagus.

Black Forest ham may be used in place of the prosciutto.

HERB MAYONNAISE

2 cups HOMEMADE
  MAYONNAISE
2 tablespoons Dijon-style
  mustard
3 tablespoons lemon juice
2 tablespoons chopped
  parsley
1 tablespoon fresh basil,
  (or ½ teaspoon dried)

2 tablespoons capers,
  drained
¼ teaspoon dry tarragon
1 teaspoon chopped
  garlic
1 teaspoon minced
  shallot

In a blender, food processor, or by hand with a whisk or wooden spoon, thoroughly blend all ingredients. Let sit several hours or overnight so that the flavors meld.

HOMEMADE MAYONNAISE

1 egg, at room temperature
1 tablespoon fresh lemon
  juice
2 teaspoons red wine
  vinegar
1 teaspoon Dijon-style
  mustard

¼ teaspoon salt
¼ teaspoon white pepper
1 cup olive or vegetable oil
  (or both)

Blend all ingredients except the oil in a blender or food processor at high speed. With the motor running, add the oil very gradually. Whip until thick. Taste for salt, pepper, and lemon and adjust if necessary.

JOHN'S MOSTACCIOLI

2 tablespoons butter

3 tablespoons olive oil,
   plus more as needed

2 large yellow onions,
   coarsely chopped

1 large green bell pepper,
   coarsely chopped

1 large red bell pepper,
   coarsely chopped

1 pound mushrooms,
   wiped clean and
   coarsely chopped

6 to 8 large, firm, ripe tomatoes,
   peeled, seeded, and
   coarsely chopped

2 tablespoons chopped garlic

½ cup dry white wine

2 tablespoons tomato paste

¼ cup chopped fresh basil,
   or 1 tablespoon dried

¼ cup chopped parsley

1 tablespoon chopped fresh
   oregano, or 1 teaspoon
   dried

⅛ teaspoon ground allspice

½ to 1 teaspoon crushed red
   pepper (optional)

2 pinches sugar
   Salt and pepper to taste

1 to 1½ cups CHICKEN STOCK,
   as needed

1 pound mostaccioli pasta

1 pound fresh, creamy
   ricotta cheese

½ pound mozzarella, grated
   Chopped parsley

1. Place a skillet over high heat; add the butter and oil and as soon as the butter melts add the onions, peppers, and mushrooms. Cook, stirring constantly, until the vegetables are limp but not brown.

2. Add the tomatoes and garlic, then the wine. Stir thoroughly to blend ingredients. Add the tomato paste, herbs, sugar, and salt and pepper to taste. Stir again. Reduce heat to moderately low and simmer, covered, for about 5 minutes. If the mixture seems too dry, add a bit of the Chicken Stock—just enough to moisten; do not turn the mixture into soup. Taste again and correct seasoning, if desired. Set aside.

3. Preheat oven to 350°.

4. In a minimum of 6 quarts of water, cook the mostaccioli according to the package directions. Cook only until the pasta is al dente; there should be a touch of chewiness still remaining. (It will be cooked further in the oven.) Drain and rinse quickly under cold water to

stop the cooking process. Toss vigorously in a colander to rid the pasta of most of the water.

5. Thoroughly combine the mostaccioli with the tomato mixture. Taste again and correct seasoning, if necessary.

6. Place the mixture in a buttered or oiled au gratin dish or appropriately sized ovenproof baking dish attractive enough to place on the table. Dot the top of the mixture with the ricotta. Sprinkle evenly with the grated mozzarella. Cover with aluminum foil and bake in preheated oven for 20 to 25 minutes, or until well heated and bubbly. Remove the foil for the last 5 minutes of baking to allow the cheese topping to harden slightly.

7. Let cool 10 to 15 minutes before serving. Sprinkle with chopped parsley.

This delicious pasta can be served as a meatless entrée for lunch or dinner or utilized as a side dish to accompany meat or poultry.

CHICKEN STOCK

Makes about 6 cups

1 (4-pound) chicken, quartered, with giblets	1 stalk celery, cut in half
1 pound veal bones, cracked	2 teaspoons salt
1 large onion, stuck with 2 cloves	Bouquet garni:
	6 sprigs parsley
2 leeks, split and washed well	2 sprigs thyme, or 1 teaspoon dried
	1 clove garlic, peeled
2 carrots, cut in half	1 bay leaf

1. Remove the skin and fat from the chicken. Place the chicken in a stock pot with the giblets, but not the liver. Add the veal bones, and 3 quarts water and bring to a boil.

2. Reduce heat to low and skim the froth that rises to the surface.

3. Add the onion, leeks, carrots, celery, salt, and bouquet garni. Simmer, skimming the froth as it rises, for 2 hours.

4. Remove the chicken from the pot. Remove the meat from the carcass

and reserve for another use. Return the carcass to the broth and simmer another 2 hours, adding boiling water as needed to keep the
ingredients covered.

5. Strain the stock, pressing the solids against the sieve to extract their
   juices. Allow to cool. Refrigerate until the fat congeals; remove the
   fat and discard. Freeze and use as needed.

The veal bones are an excellent source of gelatin.

GREEK POTATOES

6 to 8 medium-size russet
    potatoes, scrubbed
    and dried
½ cup olive oil
    Peanut oil for deep-frying
    Salt

White pepper
Greek oregano
¼ cup freshly minced parsley,
    plus more to taste
Lemon slices (optional)

1. Cube the unpeeled potatoes into ½-inch pieces and soak in ice water
   for 30 minutes to rid the potatoes of excess starch. Drain the potatoes
   and dry well on clean tea towels or paper towels.
2. In a large skillet over moderately high heat, place the olive oil and let
   it get very hot. Add the potatoes and toss constantly with a metal
   spatula until the potatoes are just beginning to turn golden brown.
   At this point, remove them from the pan and lay them in one layer
   on a cookie sheet.
3. About 30 minutes before serving, place the potatoes on the cookie
   sheet in a slow 250° oven, just to keep warm (or to rewarm).
4. Just before serving, heat the peanut oil to 400°. Deep-fry the
   potatoes for approximately 30 seconds—just enough to give them a
   golden crust. Drain and place in a heated serving bowl or on a platter.
5. Sprinkle to taste with salt, white pepper, and Greek oregano. Add ¼

cup chopped parsley and toss thoroughly. Serve, garnished with more chopped parsley and lemon slices if desired.

We have experimented with many methods of preparing Greek fries. This three-part procedure is the one that accomplishes the precise result for which we were looking: a golden, crisp potato piece, succulent inside, almost appearing to have been baked in the oven.

COSTARELLE
Marinated, Grilled Pork T-Bone

2 tablespoons finely chopped garlic	Salt
¾ cup olive oil	Freshly ground black pepper
½ cup lemon juice	4 (1½" thick) pork T-bone steaks
½ cup dry white wine (preferably vermouth)	Parsley sprigs
1 teaspoon thyme	Lemon wedges

1. Place the garlic, oil, lemon juice, wine, thyme, salt, and pepper in a bowl and whisk until the mixture congeals and thickens. Pour the mixture into a glass dish large enough to hold the steaks in one layer.
2. Place the steaks in the marinade, turning several times to thoroughly coat both sides. Let the steaks marinate for 3 to 4 hours at room temperature, turning at half-hour intervals.
3. Broil or, preferably, grill the steaks over hot, white coals for 20 minutes, turning every 5 minutes to produce a criss-cross pattern on both sides. The meat should be cooked a light grey, with a slight pinkness next to the bone.
4. Place on a large, heated serving platter or on individual heated plates. Garnish with parsley sprigs and lemon wedges.

If the steaks are overcooked, they will be dry and tough.

We purchase our pork T-bones at Don and Joe's Meats in Seattle's Pike Place Market, where you may ask for them cut "à la Adriatica." Elsewhere, simply request the pork steak cut with the loin and tenderloin left attached to the T-bone.

VEGETABLES PROVENÇAL

6 to 8 (6"-long) firm zucchini,
    scrubbed and dried
⅓ cup olive oil
1 cup coarsely chopped
    onion
2 tablespoons finely chopped
    garlic
2 cups peeled, seeded,
    and chopped tomatoes

⅓ cup dry white wine
¼ cup chopped fresh basil,
    or 2 teaspoons dried
¼ cup chopped fresh
    parsley
Salt
Freshly ground black
    pepper

1. Julienne the zucchini into 2-inch by ¼-inch strips. Heat the olive oil in a skillet over high heat. Add the zucchini strips and toss them constantly to insure even cooking. When the strips begin to get tender (3 to 4 minutes), add the onion, tomato, and garlic, continuing to stir until the onion is wilted and the tomato begins to break down.
2. Add the white wine. Stir and then add the basil, parsley, and salt and pepper to taste. Stir well and let the liquid begin to evaporate.
3. Reduce heat to low, cover the skillet, and let the mixture simmer for about 3 minutes. Taste again; correct seasoning if necessary. Place on a heated serving platter or in a heated bowl and serve.

This method of vegetable preparation is equally adaptable to green beans, broccoli, cauliflower, and small yellow summer squash. For texture and color variety, mix various vegetables.

DATES AND WALNUTS IN PHYLLO

2 cups shelled walnuts
6 cups pitted dates
½ cup good cognac
5 leaves fillo dough, at room
    temperature

½ pound butter, melted
Lightly sweetened whipped
cream

1. Process the walnuts and dates in a food processor fitted with a steel blade. When the mixture begins to stick, add the cognac. When the mixture is of a gooey, rather muddy consistency, stop mixing.
2. Refrigerate the mixture for a minimum of 1 hour or as much as 2 or 3 days, or until thoroughly chilled.
3. When chilled, remove from the refrigerator and, with your hands, roll the date/walnut mixture into long cigars no more than ½ inch in diameter. Cut the cigars into lengths as long as your index finger.
4. Carefully remove the fillo from the plastic bag and lay the pile out flat. Layer 5 sheets of fillo, one on top of the other, buttering well between each layer. Butter the top layer. Cut the sheets lengthwise in half and then twice across the width of the fillo, producing six even squares.
5. Lay the date/walnut cigars across the square at the end closest to you. Fold the sides over and roll up the date/walnut cigar in the fillo, producing another cigar-shaped roll. Butter the ends of the fillo and press lightly so that the ends stay closed. Repeat for the remaining squares.
6. Place 1 inch apart on a cookie sheet covered with waxed paper. Refrigerate for at least 1 hour (or for up to a week, covered with plastic wrap). The rolls may also be frozen at this point (in which case they can be put directly into the oven when you wish to cook them—although they may require a bit more cooking time).
7. When ready to bake, place in a preheated 500° oven and bake for 5 to 8 minutes, or until the top is nicely browned and the cigars are puffed. Top with whipped cream and serve while warm.

These are also good at room temperature and can make a delicious picnic dessert.

il Bistro

Dinner for Four

Prawns Aglio
or
Il Bistro Mussel Sauté

Linguini Sardegna

Braciole

Lemon Sorbet

Beverages:

With Prawns or Mussels and Linguini—Facelli Chardonnay

With Braciole—Barolo, Cavalotto, 1971

With or after Sorbet—Cognac, Ragnaud Estate-bottled

Peter Lamb & Frank Daquila, Owners

Frank Daquila, Head Chef

IL BISTRO

One walks into Il Bistro off Post Alley and senses the charm of entering a cafe from a street in a European city. Inside, vestiges of the Old World beckon enticingly: a rich mahogany bar, stained wood floors, creamy off-white stucco, gentle arches and curves, exposed brick, colorful kilim, and a stunning center wine table. The mood is sustained as diners are left alone to linger over food, wine and conversation, yet not feel neglected. Peter Lamb, who with Frank Daquila founded Il Bistro, insists on the expert service that heightens this intimacy: "People are coming to dine leisurely in an unpretentious but real setting—not to see the waiters."

When Peter and Frank first joined forces in 1975, their restaurant was located on the ground floor of the Harbor Heights building, now the site of Market Place North. The kitchen was makeshift, the decor less than stunning, and the menu limited. Even so, the simple, impeccably prepared food and terrific wines-by-the-glass became the talk of the town. Since its move to Pike Street in 1977, the bistro has continued to grow in the limelight of Seattle's best dining spots.

From the onset, Frank wanted the food at Il Bistro to embody the best of the lighter, more delicate Northern Italian cuisine with overtones of the zing typical of his native Abruzzi, and generally accomplished by the precise use of hot red pepper. Thus, red sauces and marinades have just the right touch of piquancy without detracting from the natural foods they accent.

The menu is always growing at Il Bistro and changes from day to day, yet consistently reflects the owners' vision of the food's ethnic style, its presentation, and the careful selection of quality ingredients. Guests are introduced to appetizers such as succulent seafood antipasto, creamy pasta, superbly sautéed prawns, or an elegant platter of prosciutto and melon. In addition to the two fresh fish entrées offered daily, one finds spicy cioppino, veal Marsala and Parmigiana (the scallopini are cut from the choicest rib eye), tenderloin sauté, and at least two pasta/seafood melanges that melt in the mouth. Il Bistro's fabulous rack of lamb ranks high among the favorites. Vegetables are not overlooked. Simple accompaniments, perfectly cooked, provide pleasing contrasts in color, flavor, and texture.

93-A Pike Street

PRAWNS AGLIO
Prawns Sautéed in Olive oil and Garlic

1 *pound shrimp*
¼ *cup olive oil*
3 *large cloves garlic,*
  finely minced
½ *teaspoon oregano*
  Salt and pepper to taste

Juice of ½ lemon
¼ *cup dry white vermouth*
  (approximately)
1 *tablespoon butter*
  Parsley sprigs
  Lemon wedges

1. Devein the shrimp with the shells on by running the blade of a small, sharp scissor down the back of the shrimp through the shell and pulling the vein out. Rinse and dry well with paper towels.
2. Heat the olive oil over high heat in a sauté pan large enough to comfortably hold all the shrimp without crowding. When the oil is hot, add the garlic and quickly stir about in the oil, taking care not to burn.
3. Immediately add the shrimp. Stir constantly. Add the oregano, a generous pinch of salt, and a generous amount of freshly ground pepper. Be sure that the garlic does not burn. As the shrimp turn pink (2 to 3 minutes), add the lemon juice. Stir thoroughly.
4. Cook only until the shrimp are pink and resilient to the touch, no more than 3 to 4 minutes. If overcooked, shrimp are tough. Place on a heated platter or individual heated serving dishes.
5. Quickly pour the vermouth into the pan, still over high heat. Let reduce by half. Add a dash of butter and a sprinkling of black pepper. Taste for seasoning and pour evenly over the shrimp. Garnish with fresh parsley and lemon wedges.

Provide your guests with large bibs and/or wet towels, for the quality of this dish is impaired if the shrimp are cooked without their shells.

Use either large (16- to 20-count per pound) or medium 25-to 32-count) shrimp. Since virtually all shrimp available in our markets have been frozen, be sure to purchase those that have been thawed only on the day you buy them, for if they have been in the case longer than that, noticeable textural and flavor damage occurs.

IL BISTRO MUSSEL SAUTÉ

1 bunch fresh basil
¼ cup olive oil
8 to 10 cloves garlic,
 finely minced
1 teaspoon dry oregano
1 pound ripe Roma or
 other fresh tomatoes,
 peeled, seeded, and diced

3 to 4 pounds fresh Atlantic
 mussels, debearded
 and scrubbed
½ cup red wine vinegar
 Freshly ground pepper
 and salt to taste
 Freshly minced parsley
 French bread

1. Wash the basil. Remove the stems. Dry the leaves with paper towels and mince.
2. Heat the oil in a large sauté pan over moderately high heat. Add the garlic, oregano and basil. Stir briskly. Just as the garlic begins to turn golden brown, add the tomatoes.
3. Cook the tomatoes, stirring constantly, for 1 minute. Add the mussels. Stir the mussels several times, turning them in the tomato mixture until they begin to open. Add the vinegar.
4. Place a lid on the pan and cook the mussels until they have completely opened. As soon as they have opened, cook 1 to 2 minutes and then remove with a slotted spoon to a heated platter. Discard any that do not open. Cover loosely with foil.
5. Reduce the liquid in the pan over high heat for 3 to 4 minutes, or until reduced by half. Add salt and pepper to taste.
6. Pour the liquid over the mussels, sprinkle with the minced parsley, and serve with crusty French bread.

Because of the vinegar, this dish is as good at room temperature as it is warm.

LINGUINI SARDEGNA

1 pint heavy cream
½ cup half and half
1 cup FRESH TOMATO
  SAUCE
1 pound Dungeness
  crabmeat
1 cup freshly grated
  Pecorini Romano cheese

1 pound egg or spinach
  linguini
¼ pound freshly grated
  Parmesan cheese
  (preferably Parmigiano-
  Reggiano)
Freshly minced parsley

1. Place the heavy cream and half and half in an enameled pan and, stirring constantly over moderately high heat, reduce the mixture until it reaches the consistency of lightly whipped cream—slightly thick and frothy.
2. Add the Fresh Tomato Sauce to the reduced cream mixture and reduce again by half over slightly lower heat.
3. Add the fresh crabmeat. When it is heated through, add the Pecorino Romano and stir until the cheese is melted.
4. Cook the linguini in 6 to 7 quarts of boiling, salted water until resistant to the bite, not mushy. Fresh linguini will only take approximately 1 minute to cook; dried, no more than 5 minutes.
5. Drain the pasta quickly and immediately place in a heated bowl. Toss the tomato/crab mixture into the pasta with swift moves of special pasta forks or other large forks and add the Parmesan while tossing.
6. Serve immediately on heated plates or in heated bowls. Sprinkle with minced parsley.

Note: The only trick to making successful pasta dishes is to be organized, because once the pasta hits the water, the dish is near completion. Before making a quick pasta sauce, be sure to turn the pasta water on high, as it will take 10 to 15 minutes for it to boil. Have your tossing and serving bowls or plates heated, as pasta cools quickly enough as it is. As importantly, get your guests organized and ready to eat before adding the pasta to the water.

With succulent Dungeness crab available in this area, Linguini Sardegna takes on a special essence. Other types of crab could be used. The combination of fresh cream, reduced to a velvety consistency, and tasty homemade tomato sauce contributes to the rich yet clean flavor of this dish.

FRESH TOMATO SAUCE

5 pounds fresh, ripe pear tomatoes,

1 bunch fresh basil, leaves removed from stems, rinsed, dried with paper towels and finely minced

2 tablespoons olive oil

1 small onion, finely chopped

8 to 10 cloves garlic, finely minced

½ cup dry white wine
   Salt and freshly ground pepper to taste

1. Cut the stem tips from the tomatoes. Place in a large pan with water to cover. Cover and bring to a boil over high heat. Cook until the skins crack, about 4 to 5 minutes.
2. Drain in a colander. Rinse with cold water, then squeeze the pulp out of the skins and into a bowl. Crush by hand and set aside.
3. Heat a heavy-bottomed saucepan over high heat. Add the oil and allow to heat. Add the onion, garlic, and basil and sauté for 3 to 4 minutes.
4. Add the wine and cook 1 to 2 minutes. Add the crushed tomatoes and salt and pepper to taste. Continue cooking over moderately high heat for 10 to 15 minutes.

This sauce should have a fresh, clean taste, sufficiently salted, but not heavily spiced. Use the extra sauce in other Italian or fresh vegetable dishes immediately or freeze in small containers and use as needed.

BRACIOLE
Stuffed Beef Roll

2- to 2½-pound round steak,
    butterflied
    Grated rind of 1 lemon
    Salt and pepper
2½ teaspoons oregano
¼ pound prosciutto,
    thinly sliced
2 cups bread crumbs
¼ pound Parmigiano-
    Reggiano cheese, grated
½ cup chopped parsley

½ teaspoon rosemary
½ cup flour
¼ cup olive oil
4 cloves garlic, finely
    chopped
1 small onion, diced
½ cup dry red wine
2 cups chopped, canned
    pear tomatoes
    with their juice

1. Open the butterflied steak and, with waxed paper covering it, pound evenly with a meat mallet until approximately ¼ inch thick. Rub the lemon rind, salt, pepper and 1½ teaspsoons oregano into the meat.
2. Lay the prosciutto slices evenly on the steak. Sprinkle the bread crumbs, grated Parmesan, and parsley evenly over the prosciutto slices.
3. Roll the braciole tightly, taking care while rolling to tuck in both ends so as to hold in the filling while cooking. Tie the roll with strings at 1½- to 2-inch intervals.
4. Rub the rosemary between your palms to break it up. Season the flour with the rosemary, remaining oregano, and salt and pepper. Rub this mixture onto the surface of the beef roll.
5. In a pan large enough to hold the roll, heat the olive oil over moderately high heat. Add the beef roll, turning to brown the entire surface.
6. Add the garlic and onion and cook until the garlic begins to turn golden brown. Add the wine and cook for 1 minute.
7. Add the tomatoes with their juice and salt and pepper to taste. Cover the pan and simmer over low heat for 1 to 1½ hours, or until very tender when pierced with a fork. If liquid appears to be

diminishing during the cooking, splash a bit more wine into the pan.

8. Remove from the pan and place on a heated platter. Remove the strings, cut into ½-inch thick slices, pour the tomato mixture over the slices, and serve.

Note: If serving cold, place the braciole on a platter, pour the sauce over it, cover tightly with plastic wrap or foil, and refrigerate. Before serving, bring to room temperature, remove the strings, and cut into slices as mentioned above. The slices can be served on a bed of lettuce, accompanied by freshly baked bread.

This scrumptious roll is equally good hot or cold.

LEMON SORBET

1½ cups fresh lemon juice
3 cups SIMPLE SYRUP

1 tablespoon grated lemon zest

Combine the ingredients and freeze in an ice-cream maker, or place in a bowl set within a larger bowl holding ice cubes and salted water. Beat the mixture with a portable mixer or wire whisk for several minutes until it begins to be thoroughly chilled. Cover and place in the freezer until frozen, stirring occasionally.

SIMPLE SYRUP

2 cups sugar

4 cups water

Place the sugar and water in a stainless steel or enameled saucepan and boil for 5 minutes. Strain through a sieve lined with a damp cloth. Cool.

BOONDOCK'S SUNDECKER'S & GREENTHUMB'S

Dinner for Six

Stuffed Mushrooms

Greenthumb's Garden Delight Salad

Paella

Chocolate Mousse

Wine:

Rosé d'Anjou, M. Monmousseau,
or
Meursault, Ropiteau Frères,
or
Puligny-Montrachet, Labouré-Roi

Gerry Kingen, Owner

David Madayag, Corporate Executive Chef

Burt Blackmore, House Chef

Nestled among small shops featuring antiques, groceries, clothing and quick foods, Boondock's opened in 1973 in what was then a deteriorating neighborhood. Thirty-year old Gerry Kingen, the owner, and his partner Donovan Stangle wanted a sundeck, a myriad of light, airy plants, and a tremendously diversified menu of well-prepared food in their new establishment in the "boondocks." Boondock's Sundecker's & Greenthumb's, with its open kitchen, friendly staff and casually elegant atmosphere was an instant success.

In 1978 Gerry Kingen purchased his partner's share of the Boondock's Corporation and now, as president, is committed to keeping Boondock's of the same quality and character his loyal patrons have enjoyed. Gerry Kingen says, "Boondock's is a landmark in Seattle. I plan to continue to meet the value/price ratio for our customers, to serve consistently good food, and to maintain the unique environment with sincere, warm, personal service."

In addition to Boondock's, Gerry Kingen owns the Red Robin Burger and Spirits Emporiums, featuring 28 different kinds of hamburgers; Lion O's Paradise Rock Cafe, with its mammoth, hand-carved mahogany bar from the old Marcus Daly Hotel in Anaconda, Montana, and fresh East Coast lobster flown in daily; Lake Union Cafe, featuring a daily seafood "fresh sheet," an espresso bar and a resplendent view of Lake Union; Portland, Oregon's Salty Pickerel's and Angus McHereford's; and a Salty's in Redondo Beach. The newest member of the Kingen family of restaurants is yet another Salty's, this time located in Alki.

For Gerry Kingen, the constant challenge to try something new and different in his restaurants has made business a pleasure. Out of this "new and different" philosophy arises the most current renovation at Boondock's: the already vast menu is presently undergoing modifications which will very likely result in "the largest menu in Seattle, with over 150 entrées."

It has been mentioned more than once that a Capitol Hill real estate firm said, a year after Boondock's opened and Broadway was once again a growing, exciting street of business, that it was a restaurant "so good it saved a neighborhood." It is worth repeating again because it is probably true.

611 Broadway East

BOONDOCK'S

STUFFED MUSHROOMS

18 jumbo mushroom caps
6 tablespoons butter
Juice of 1 lemon
¼ cup white wine
12 ounces hot Roma sausage
½ small onion, diced
½ green pepper, diced
8 ounces asiago cheese,
   shredded (Parmesan
   may be substituted)

1½ teaspoons oregano
2 ounces chicken stock
Dash Worcestershire
   sauce
¾ ounce fresh garlic purée or
   minced garlic

1. Wash mushrooms and remove stems. Sauté in butter, lemon and wine. Allow to cool.

2. Bake sausage in a 350° oven for 10 minutes. Cool.

3. Grind sausage with the onion and green pepper.

4. Add 4 ounces asiago cheese to the sausage mixture, then add the remaining ingredients, mixing well.

5. Cook the sausage mixture on medium heat for 10 minutes, stirring constantly. Cool.

6. Stuff sautéed mushrooms with cooled sausage mixture and bake at 350° for approximately 10 minutes. Top with remaining 4 ounces of asiago cheese and heat under the broiler until the cheese melts.

GREENTHUMB'S GARDEN DELIGHT SALAD

1½ heads romaine
1 large cucumber
1 large zucchini
1 yellow squash
3 carrots
3 stalks celery
¼ pound small mushrooms
2 cups alfalfa sprouts, packed

2 tomatoes, each cut into 6 wedges
½ cup black olives, drained
1 medium broccoli flower
1 small cauliflower
DRESSING
6 ounces mozzarella cheese, coarsely shredded

1. Wash the romaine and remove the outer leaves. Cut the romaine into bite-size pieces and place in individual salad bowls—not plates.
2. French cut (long elliptical slices) the cucumber, zucchini, squash, carrots and celery. Wash the mushrooms and pat dry. Break broccoli and cauliflower into flowerettes.
3. Toss all the vegetables together with the DRESSING but without the romaine. Arrange vegetables artistically atop romaine and pour remaining DRESSING over. Sprinkle salads with shredded cheese.

DRESSING

½ cup red wine vinegar
1 cup olive oil
2 tablespoons whole capers
1 tablespoon Dijon mustard
1 tablespoon lemon juice
½ teaspoon dry mustard
2 teaspoons Worcestershire sauce

½ teaspoon garlic powder
1 teaspoon salt
¼ teaspoon pepper
½ teaspoon oregano
¼ teaspoon basil
½ teaspoon parsley
¼ teaspoon thyme
¼ teaspoon tarragon

Mix all ingredients well in a mixing bowl. Do not use a blender because the capers should be whole.

PAELLA

3 cups chicken broth
   Pinch saffron
1½ cups rice
6 ounces diced hot Roma
   sausage
10 ounces chicken drummets,
   wings or small legs
6 ounces diced ham
12 ounces fresh clams,
   cleaned

12 ounces fresh mussels,
   cleaned
1 pound King crab sections
12 ounces scallops, rinsed
10 ounces fresh diced cod
12 ounces prawns, shelled,
   deveined
8 ounces peas
4 ounces diced pimientos

1. Prepare a strong chicken broth, adding to it the small amount of saffron. Cook the rice in the broth and set aside.

2. Place the sausage in a large pan and brown it thoroughly. Using a little hot oil in the pan should keep the sausage from sticking.

3. Add the chicken, then the ham. Continue cooking as you add the clams, mussels and crab. Stirring and cooking, add the scallops, cod and prawns. Finally, add the peas and pimientos.

4. Sauté the entire mixture for about 4 minutes, checking especially the scallops for doneness.

5. Add the cooked rice, mixing in carefully. Serve piping hot.

Paella is undoubtedly the most famous of all authentic Spanish dishes. In Spain, the truly glorious paella is cooked over a pine fire in a special paella pan, and burning sticks have to be added and taken away to lower and increase the heat as the cooking demands. Unlike our sautéed version here at Boondock's, the true paella is cooked all at the same time—the rice, flesh and vegetables all fresh and raw at the outset. Depending on the region, the true paella may include rabbit, chicken, prawns, clams, snails, mussels, eel, squid, crawfish, various sausages, vegetables, herbs and seasonings. In every recipe I've seen, saffron is faithfully included. Boondock's paella, in my opinion, geographically speaking and all, is a fine tribute to the real thing.

CHOCOLATE MOUSSE

4 ounces semi-sweet
    chocolate
2 cups plus 2 tablespoons
    whipping cream

3 tablespoons brandy
½ cup sugar
½ cup egg whites

1. Melt chocolate and 2 tablespoons whipping cream in a double boiler.
2. In a heavy saucepan, make a simple syrup with brandy and sugar.
3. Combine the chocolate with the simple syrup and let cool completely.
4. Whip the egg whites until stiff and add the chocolate mixture.
5. Beat 2 cups whipping cream until stiff, and add the chocolate-egg white mixture to the whipped cream by folding gently.
6. Spoon into chilled glasses and chill. Decorate with whipped cream, using a pastry bag.

The 41 page Boondock's menu is constantly being changed and improved. Gerry Kingen himself writes most of the descriptive material about the food items and personally knows what is in each and how it should be prepared.

≈ BRASSERIE PITTSBOURG ≈

Dinner for Four

Potage aux Concombres

Oysters Baked with Horseradish Butter Sauce

Volaille aux Pommes

Pilaf of Rice Mediterranean

Salade Pavillon

Coupe Pavillon

Wine:

With Soup—semi-dry Graves from France or dry Sherry

With Oysters—Riesling or Gewürztraminer from
Washington, California or France

With Chicken—hard cider or red Burgundy

With Dessert—Sauternes or Asti Spumante

Francois and Julia Kissel, Owners

Francois Kissel, Head Chef

BRASSERIE PITTSBOURG

J ulia Kissel describes all great chefs as being artistic, creative, cultured, sensitive and musical; she says that they possess great energy, sense of humor, love of gardens and show kindness toward others. "Francois is akin to the great chefs of the world. He is the only classically trained Parisian chef in this region."

When Julia and Francois Kissel discovered that the Pittsburgh Lunch and Cafeteria, Seattle's oldest restaurant, was for sale, they bought it quickly, cleaned and scrubbed it thoroughly, and opened their Brasserie Pittsbourg on October 1, 1969. It was an immediate success. In their Brasserie the Kissels retained the white tile floors, the pressed tin ceiling, and the antique tables and chairs. They added collector's prints for the walls, fresh plants and dried flower arrangements, and magnificent 17th century copper pieces for decoration, many of which had been their own wedding gifts. And Francois cooked. He was quickly recognized for his mastery of the French classics and for his innovative and imaginative personal contributions to the menu.

In August of 1975, the Kissels opened their second restaurant in the Pioneer Square area, City Loan Pavillon. The new setting and menu inspired Francois to experiment with nouvelle cuisine, giving vent to his creativity. In April of 1985, the Kissels decided to combine these two initial restaurants and have relocated. The new restaurant, whose name of Brasserie Pavillon reflects the compilation process, retains the best qualities of both, including the Travel/Holiday Award.

Maximilien in the Market, the Kissel's other restaurant, opened in its present location in the Public Market in 1978. "It is a unique restaurant," says Julia, "because it is the last real public market in the United States and the menu is based on French market food." The chairs and tables are from nineteenth century England, as are the lovely fruitwood mirrors which reflect the whole harbor scene and the mountains beyond the city to the south. Francois, when sitting in Maximilien, feels as if he is "in a French restaurant overlooking the Seine."

Francois says that "cooking, like music, is an art. To be a great chef, you have the basics taught by the masters with a classic approach, but from that point there is no limit to what you can do. Cooking is an art only when you can be creative and imaginative."

206 1st Avenue South
81-A Pike Street

BRASSERIE PITTSBOURG

POTAGE AUX CONCOMBRES
Cucumber Soup

4 medium cucumbers
4 tablespoons butter
1 cup chopped leeks
1 cup chopped onion
1 cup diced raw potatoes
6 cups chicken stock

Salt and pepper
1 tablespoon chopped
   parsley
1 tablespoon chopped chives
1 tablespoon chopped fresh
   chervil

1. Peel, seed and dice cucumbers.
2. Sauté chopped leeks and onions in butter. When cooked through, add cucumbers and potatoes. Sauté 3 minutes, then add stock and simmer for 20 minutes more. Season to taste with salt and pepper.
3. When ready to serve, garnish with herbs.

This soup can be served cold and then garnished with a few thin slices of cucumbers, one or two slices of hard-cooked eggs, and a dollop of sour cream.

OYSTERS BAKED WITH HORSERADISH BUTTER SAUCE

12 large oysters
1 tablespoon grated
   horseradish
Juice of 1 lemon
1 cup salted butter
2 tablespoons chopped
   shallots

1 teaspoon Dijon mustard
Pinch sugar
Pepper
Chopped parsley
   to garnish

1. Open oysters in hot oven, being sure not to overcook.
2. Lift and discard upper shells.

3. Mix all other ingredients in a saucepan until butter is melted. Spoon over oysters.

4. Bake in hot oven 3 to 4 minutes. Decorate with chopped parsley when serving.

These oysters could be cooked in an open fire on the beach or in the fireplace in the winter. The sauce is served lukewarm and spooned over each oyster as you eat it. This dish also makes a marvelous hors d'oeuvre or appetizer and was created by Francois for Julia Child and Company during a short stay at a beach cottage.

VOLAILLE AUX POMMES
Chicken with Apples

2 tablespoons chopped shallots	2 whole medium breasts of chicken, halved
3 tablespoons butter	1 cup chicken stock
½ teaspoon curry powder	4 apples, peeled, cored, and quartered
Pinch thyme	
Pinch tarragon	1 tablespoon cornstarch
1 clove garlic, chopped	1 cup sweet vermouth
1 tablespoon salt	

1. Sauté shallots lightly in butter.

2. Add curry, herbs, garlic and salt. Mix together and coat the 4 pieces of chicken with the mixture.

3. Bake in a 400° oven for 7 to 8 minutes.

4. Add chicken stock and apples. Bake 5 minutes more. Deglaze with cornstarch diluted in the vermouth.

5. Bake again until the apples are tender and the chicken is done, 5 minutes or more.

6. When serving, pour apples and sauce over the chicken.

One could also use medium-ripe pears, peaches or nectarines during their season.

PILAF OF RICE MEDITERRANEAN

1 cup long grain rice
1 cup vermicelli
4 tablespoons butter

Salt and pepper
½ to 1 cup raisins

1. Cook rice as you usually would. Cook vermicelli in boiling salted water al dente.
2. Mix rice and vermicelli with butter. Add salt and pepper to taste. Add raisins to taste.

This can be prepared a day before and reheated in a double boiler.

SALADE PAVILLON

1 cup finely diced potatoes
½ head romaine
1 head Bibb lettuce

Fresh herbs, such as
French tarragon,
chervil, sweet basil,
chives or mint
DRESSING

1. Boil finely diced potatoes till tender, yet still slightly crisp. Cool.
2. Clean greens and tear into bite-size pieces.
3. Toss greens and potatoes with Dressing. Sprinkle generously with minced fresh herbs.

DRESSING

1 teaspoon lemon juice
1 teaspoon vinegar
1 teaspoon Dijon mustard
½ teaspoon salt

Freshly ground pepper
1 tablespoon olive oil
3 tablespoons peanut, or
other salad oil

1. Combine all ingredients except the oils, mixing well.

2. Add oils and whisk or use a blender to emulsify.

One could garnish with chopped olives, or better yet, truffles, to make the salad very classy.

COUPE PAVILLON

1 cup fresh or frozen
   raspberries
2 tablespoons sugar
1 teaspoon fresh lemon juice
1 tablespoon Kirsch
4 scoops vanilla ice cream

6 macaroons, crumbled
1 tablespoon finely chopped
   candied lemon, orange
   or lime peel
1 tablespoon Grand
   Marnier

1. Sieve raspberries to get maximum juice. Mix with sugar, lemon juice and Kirsch.
2. In large individual glasses, put a scoop of ice cream and then apportion the raspberry sauce on top. Sprinkle with crumbled macaroons.
3. Combine chopped candied fruit peel with Grand Marnier and sprinkle on top of macaroons.

Blackberries, boysenberries or loganberries could easily be substituted, or if one should have them, black currants. This is an easy dessert one can make any time of the year, especially if using home-frozen berries.

I grew up in a family where food was part of the grace of life. My father was a high official in the French government, and we led a very social life. The kitchen was a wonderful place to be, but to stay there, you had to make yourself useful. I watched, tasted, copied my parents, and learned a great deal.

At 18 I began training to be a chef. I studied at the Hotel Restaurant School in Paris and apprenticed at two of the best restaurants in the city.

CAFE JUANITA

Dinner for Four

Insalata di Frutti di Mare

Spaghettini with Smoked Salmon

Pan-Braised Sea Bass

Mixed Fresh Vegetables with Parmesan Cheese

Cafe Juanita Green Salad with Herbed Vinaigrette

Spuma di Cioccolata

Beverages:

*As an apéritif or with the Insalata or Spaghettini—
Italian Spumanti Cartizze or Pro Secco*

With Insalata and Spaghettini—Orvieto Classico, Decugano dei Barbi

With Sea Bass—Pinot Grìgio, J. Brigl

With Cioccolata—Vin Santo

Peter Dow, Proprietor

Nancy Varriale, Chef

CAFE JUANITA

Peter Dow, proprietor of the Cafe Juanita and long-standing restaurateur in the Seattle area, wants people to have fun when they come to his dining establishment. Considering his own experiences in Italy, in combination with his already existing personal philosophy about eating, Peter encourages "life and fun at the Italian table. Eating a meal is more than just dining; it is an event where people converse, laugh, and relax." This attitude is combined with the absolute commitment to quality and simplicity: simplicity in the decor, in the service, and in the food. The current site is warm and comforting in its clean, crisp presentation.

The Cafe Juanita had humble beginnings in 1978. The original cafe, serving only breakfast and lunch, was in essence just an extension of Peter's infamous Gordo's hamburger stand, which he owned at that time. In 1979, Peter began researching and experimenting with Northern Italian food. Soon fresh pasta, *pollo ai pistacci* lasagne, and a fresh fish daily special followed on the dinner menu. Then came an enthusiastic review in the *Argus* and, by the autumn of 1979, Peter Dow had an earthy but tremendously successful little Italian restaurant.

A few years later, Peter traveled to Italy, where he observed cooking and eating styles. In December, 1981, he returned to open the present Cafe Juanita. The pasta at Cafe Juanita is still rolled by hand on an Atlas machine each day, and one will always find a fresh, authentic Italian fish dish on the menu among other selections of lamb, veal, rabbit, and beef preparations. Fresh steamed vegetables and salad accompany all entrées, which are followed by assorted desserts and espresso.

Cafe Juanita now harbors a small winery in the basement of the premises, thus becoming the first restaurant in Washington to produce and sell its own wines. Cavatappi, as the establishment dubs itself, specializes in Sauvignon Blanc, and enables the restaurant to offer one of the best wine lists in the state. With over 250 Italian wines available, Cafe Juanita has recently been named one of six in the state to receive the Wine Spectator Award. Just as consistency in quality and presentation is the ever-present goal for each dish that leaves the kitchen, here, too, excellence is the object.

9702 Northeast 120th Place
Kirkland

INSALATA DI FRUTTI DE MARE

4 pounds fresh mussels
2 pounds fresh steamer
   clams
   Olive oil
1 pound scallops, cut into
   bite-size pieces,
   if necessary
1 pound squid, cleaned,
   cut into rings, and
   thoroughly dried

1½ pounds cooked octopus
   meat
1½ pounds cooked bay shrimp
   Juice of 2 lemons (more
   as needed)
2 teaspoons Dijon-style
   mustard
   Salt and pepper to taste
¼ cup finely chopped
   fresh parsley

1. Debeard the mussels and rinse well under cold running water. Rinse the clams. Coat the bottom of a large, covered frying pan or pot with the olive oil, heat over moderately high heat, and place the mussels and clams in the pan. Cover and cook over high heat just until they open. Discard any that do not open within 5 minutes.

2. Remove the mussels and clams from the frying pan. When cool enough to handle, remove the meats from the shells and place in a large mixing bowl. Reserve the pan juices, straining through damp cheesecloth if there appears to be grit in the liquid.

3. Wipe the pan dry and coat lightly again with olive oil. Quickly sauté the scallops. Remove the scallops from the pan the moment they go from translucent to opaque, 1 minute or less. Put them in the bowl with the mussels and clams.

4. With the pan still on moderately high heat, add the squid rings and sauté for 15 to 20 seconds only. Remove the squid and place in the bowl with the other cooked seafood.

5. Cut the tentacles away from the body of the octopus and slice into thin circles. Place the octopus meat in the bowl. Add the shrimp meat.

6. In a smaller bowl, place the lemon juice, mustard, salt, and pepper. Gradually add ¼ cup olive oil, whisking until well-combined. Taste for tartness. Much of the lemon will be readily absorbed by the seafood, so the dressing should be rather tart. Whisk in ¼ cup of the reserved mussel and clam broth.

7. Pour the dressing over the seafood in the large mixing bowl. Add the chopped parsley. Mix well and taste again. Add more lemon, mustard, salt, and/or pepper, if desired. Let the salad marinate for a minimum of 3 to 4 hours. Serve at room temperature—not icy cold.

Note: "Green," or uncooked, shrimp in the shell can be used in place of the already-cooked bay shrimp meat. In this case, cut down the back of the shrimp with a small scissors, thus allowing for the vein removal while leaving the shell on. Dry and then sauté in the pan in the same manner as the scallops and squid, removing the shrimp the moment they turn pink. When cool enough to handle, simply pull off the shells and add the shrimp to the other ingredients.

This salad may conveniently be made a day ahead.

SPAGHETTINI WITH SMOKED SALMON

2 *cups heavy cream*
2 *tablespoons butter*
¼ *pound Nova-style lox,
    finely chopped*
3 *ounces Parmesan cheese,
    grated
    Freshly ground black
    pepper to taste*

1 *tablespoon salt*
1 *pound fresh or dried
    spaghettini pasta
    Chopped fresh parsley
    (optional)*

1. Place 5 to 6 quarts water in a large cooking pot and place, covered, over high heat. Allow to come to a full rolling boil.
2. Meanwhile, combine the cream and butter in a medium enameled skillet or saucepan. Bring to a boil and reduce until thickened enough to easily coat a spoon.
3. Add the salmon and 2 ounces of the Parmesan cheese. Stir until well mixed. Season to taste with pepper.
4. When the water comes to a boil, add the salt and, all at once, the pasta. Stir two or three times with a large pasta fork and cook until the spaghettini is softened but still slightly resistant to the bite (al dente). Fresh spaghettini will take only 2 to 3 minutes; packaged dry spaghettini will take up to 5 minutes.

5. Drain the pasta immediately in a colander; do not rinse. As soon as it is well drained, place in a warm bowl and pour on the cream/salmon mixture. Toss thoroughly and quickly. Dish the portions into heated serving bowls, top with more grated Parmesan, and serve immediately, garnished with a bit of chopped fresh parsley if desired.

PAN-BRAISED SEA BASS

1 *cup white flour*
1 *teaspoon basil*
1 *teaspoon dill weed*
1 *teaspoon thyme*
4 *(6- to 8-ounce) filets of
   sea bass*
4 *tablespoons butter*

1 *lemon, halved,
   seeds removed*
1 *tablespoon capers,
   rinsed and drained*
Lemon wedges
Parsley sprigs

1. Combine the flour, basil, dill weed, and thyme. Dry the fillets impeccably with paper towels and dust with the seasoned flour. This can be done ahead, in which case lay the fillets side by side, not piled on each other, on a platter; cover lightly and place in the refrigerator until ready to sauté.

2. Over medium heat, melt the butter in a frying pan large enough to hold the fillets without crowding them. Put the belly side in the butter first (as this will be the presentation side on the plate) and the skin side up. (The skinned side will always have a darker color than the belly side.)

3. Cover the fillets immediately and then let braise in the butter over medium heat until the edges turn opaque. At this point, turn the fish. Squeeze with the lemon juice to taste and sprinkle the capers on and around the fish.

4. Cover again and cook for only 2 to 3 minutes, or until the fish flakes easily when a fork or knife tip is inserted into one of the muscle rings. There should be a slight line of pinkness in the very center of the fillet, as it will continue to cook for up to 1 minute after being removed from the heat.

5. Place on heated plates. Serve with lemon wedges and sprigs of parsley.

Red snapper, cod, halibut, perch, or sole can also be used.

MIXED FRESH VEGETABLES WITH PARMESAN CHEESE

6 cups freh mixed
  vegetables of choice
Juice of ½ lemon

5 tablespoons melted butter
½ cup grated Parmesan
  cheese

1. Cut the vegetables, after having rinsed them thoroughly, into consistent sizes. If using vegetables that require slightly different cooking times, isolate them from each other so that the harder vegetables can be added to the steamer first, with the others following at appropriate intervals.
2. Place 1 inch water in the bottom of a vegetable steamer and bring the water to a boil over high heat. Place the vegetables in the steamer and, with the lid on, proceed with steaming the vegetables until they are done to your liking. Nutritional value will be retained if the vegetables are cooked to the al dente stage—slightly soft, but having a pleasant crunch.
3. Remove the vegetables from the steamer and place in a heated serving bowl. Squeeze the lemon juice over them, drizzle with the melted butter, and sprinkle on the Parmesan cheese. Toss to coat the vegetables evenly and serve.

Yellow squash, zucchini, broccoli, green beans, asparagus, fennel, cauliflower, and Brussels sprouts are recommended in any combination.

CAFE JUANITA GREEN SALAD WITH HERBED VINAIGRETTE

1 egg yolk
Juice of 1 lemon
2 tablespoons white wine
  vinegar
Pinch of cayenne
Pinch of salt
¾ to 1 cup olive oil

1 to 2 teaspoons minced fresh
  herbs (marjoram,
  oregano, basil, chives,
  tarragon, parsley)
2 to 3 quarts fresh, crisp greens,
  thoroughly rinsed and
  dried with paper towels
  or in a salad spinner

1. Place the first five ingredients in a small bowl. Whisk constantly while adding the olive oil to taste. (Less oil will produce a more vinegary taste.) Whisk in the minced herbs.
2. Rinse the greens thoroughly and dry with paper towels or in a salad spinner. Tear into salad pieces.
3. Drizzle the dressing over the greens and toss to thoroughly coat each leaf.

If the leaves of greens are not thoroughly dry, the dressing will not adhere properly to the surfaces, resulting in a flavorless salad with all the dressing sitting in a puddle at the bottom of the bowl.

SPUMA DI CIOCCOLATA

4 ounces sweet chocolate
  (or 3 ounces semi-sweet
  chocolate and 1 ounce
  butter
2 tablespoons brewed
  espresso or strong coffee

¼ cup dark rum
¼ cup sugar
4 eggs, separated
2 cups heavy cream
  Shaved chocolate

1. Melt the chocolate with the coffee in a small pan that is sitting over boiling water. Stir until smooth; set aside.
2. Make a syrup of the rum and sugar by mixing them together in a small saucepan and boiling the mixture for 1 minute.
3. After letting the syrup cool for a few moments, whisk it into the egg yolks in a medium-size bowl, beating until thick.
4. Add the melted chocolate to the egg yolk mixture.
5. In a separate, clean bowl, beat the egg whites until stiff. Fold into the chocolate mixture. Allow the mixture to cool.
6. In another clean bowl, beat the cream until stiff and fold it into the chocolate mixture. Make sure the cream and chocolate are well blended.
7. Place the Spuma di Cioccolata in sherbet or parfait glasses and top with shaved chocolate. Chill until ready to serve.

COSTAS OPA

Dinner for Six

Saganaki

Horiatiki Salad

Greek Beef Souvlaki

Rice Pilaf

Tzatziki

Galaktoboureko

Wine:

With Saganaki and/or Salad—Kokineli, or Retsina, or Santa Laura

With Souvlaki—red Demestica or Sanielis

Costas Antonopoulos, Owner & Chef

COSTAS OPA

A peculiar homesickness can beset travelers returned from Greece. Thoughts of the coastline, the laughter, dancing, and noshing in tavernas, the flaky, buttery pastries, the aromatic souvlaki stands, the fresh salads and feta in olive oil and vinegar, the creamy, herb-imbued casseroles—all urge a longing to catch the earliest plane to Athens. Aware that these images have become vital to memories, and nostalgic himself, Costas Antonopoulos created the next best thing to being there: Costas Opa.

Costas Opa, which crosses a Greek taverna with a formal restaurant, makes reminiscing a pleasure. Tantalizing odors accost the entering guest, and one can see food displayed behind glass dividers. Greek music, Greek fabrics and rugs, pottery, white stucco, and hanging copper enhance the mood and complete the setting.

Yet, Costas' primary concern is not to offer an ersatz return; it is, instead, to serve authentic Greek food and classic Greek wines. One may recall warm evenings on a terrace, sipping retsina and leisurely scooping up taramosalata, melizanosalata, hummos and tzatziki with warm pita bread. The traditional saganaki cheese appetizer, which is flamed with a brandy and then doused with squeezes of fresh lemon right at the table, is an old favorite. And if not too filled with feta cheese, olives, and peppers, one can take on the entrées with gusto: dolmades, gyros, moussaka, kalamari, spanakopita, roast lamb, herbed chicken, paidakia, lemonátho, or the aromatic souvlaki of either lamb or beef, as the customer desires. Costas Opa also makes available a large variety of good, inexpensive Greek wines to accompany its ever-so-tempting meals.

Costas still does much of the cooking and spends hours in the kitchen supervising the quality of prepared dishes. He came to the United States in 1968, after spending a year in Vancouver, B.C., and since has worked exclusively in the restaurant business. After establishing two other restaurants, Costas has strived for, and has achieved, excellence at Costas Opa since its opening in 1981.

3400 Fremont North

SAGANAKI

18 ounces Kafalotyri or
    Pecorino Romano cheese
3 large eggs, lightly beaten
    Flour
3 to 4 tablespoons olive oil

1½ tablespoons Metaxa brandy
    Lemon wedges
    Chopped fresh parsley
    Pita or any crusty bread

1. In a warm oven, preheat a serving dish that is able to withstand and retain heat. It must get warm enough to heat the brandy for flambéing.
2. Slice the cheese into even pieces ¼ inch thick, preferably triangles or squares. Dip into the beaten eggs and dredge in flour to coat well.
3. Heat the olive oil over medium heat in a heavy-bottomed skillet large enough to hold all the cheese. When hot, place the coated cheese pieces in the pan and fry on one side until golden brown.
4. Turn with a spatula and fry about 1 minute. Transfer, browned side up, to the heated serving dish. Take immediately to the table.
5. Pour the brandy over and, keeping the dish away from your hair, ignite with a match. At this point it is important to shout "Opa!" very loudly.
6. When the flames die out, squeeze 1 or 2 lemon wedges over the cheese. Garnish with the chopped parsley and remaining lemon wedges and serve with pita or other bread.

HORIATIKI SALAD

6 tomatoes
3 cucumbers
1 onion
1 green bell pepper
½ pound feta cheese
¾ cup olive oil
    (approximately)

¼ cup red wine vinegar
    (approximately)
    Salt and freshly ground
    black pepper
12 peperoncini (optional)
18 to 24 Greek olives

1. Dice the tomatoes in ½-inch cubes. Peel and dice the cucumbers in ½-inch cubes. Place in a large salad bowl.
2. Slice the onion and bell pepper into 12 thin rings each; quarter the rings and add to the salad.
3. Slice the feta cheese about ¼ inch thick. Crumble over the salad.
4. Sprinkle the olive oil over, followed by about ¼ cup vinegar or to taste. Salt lightly and grind fresh pepper over. Toss until well coated.
5. Taste for seasoning. Add more vinegar if tartness is lacking; add more oil if too tart. Divide among six plates or bowls. Garnish with the peperoncini, if desired, and the olives.

This salad is most superb when made with vine-ripened tomatoes, garden cucumbers, and sweet, tender onions. In any case, be sure to select firm but ripe tomatoes for the best result.

GREEK BEEF SOUVLAKI

2 pounds beef sirloin tip or tenderloin	1 bell pepper, cut in 1" squares
4 large cloves garlic, minced	Salt to taste
½ cup olive oil	Parsley sprigs
¼ cup dry white wine	Lemon wedges
⅛ teaspoon black pepper	Cherry tomatoes
1 tablespoon Greek oregano	
1 large onion, cut in eighths and separated	

1. Remove all the fat and connective tissue from the meat. Cut in 1-inch cubes and place in a bowl large enough to hold it with enough room to gently toss in the marinade.
2. Add the garlic, olive oil, white wine, pepper, and oregano. Toss to coat the meat evenly and thoroughly. The onion and pepper may, optionally, be marinated with the meat. Store the mixture overnight, well covered, in the refrigerator.

3. Skewer the meat with the onion and pepper, 1 piece of onion between each piece of meat, with perhaps only 1 or 2 pieces of pepper on each skewer. Reserve the marinade for basting. Lay the skewers on a plate, cover, and return to the refrigerator.

4. Remove the skewers from the refrigerator about 15 minutes before serving time. Preheat grill, broiler, or frying pan. If using the broiler, place the skewers on a cookie sheet or pan large enough to hold without crowding. If using a frying pan, preheat over moderately high heat. Cook, turning twice and salting and basting with the reserved marinade each time, for 7 to 12 minutes or until done to taste.

5. Remove to a heated platter. Garnish with parsley, lemon wedges, and cherry tomatoes. Serve with Rice Pilaf and Tzatziki.

One of the keys to tender, succulent souvlaki—in addition to the quality of meat used—is to not salt the meat until it is cooking.

RICE PILAF

¼ cup olive oil
1 small onion, diced small
1 cup long-grain rice
2 cups hot CHICKEN STOCK
  (see page 6), canned
  chicken broth, or bouillon

⅛ teaspoon salt
  (approximately)
2 tablespoons butter

1. Heat the olive oil in a heavy-bottomed skillet over moderately high heat. Add the onion and cook for 4 to 5 minutes, or until softened and lightly browned.

2. Add the rice and cook, stirring constantly, for 3 minutes; towards the end of this time you should hear a crackling sound.

3. Add the hot stock, salt, and butter. If the stock is not very salty, you may wish to add more salt. Stir once or twice. Place the lid on the pan as soon as the liquid comes to a boil. Reduce heat to low and

cook for 15 to 20 minutes, testing at 15 minutes to see if all the liquid has been absorbed and the grains are separated and sufficiently cooked.

4. Stir gently and remove to a heated serving dish.

As a result of the rice absorbing the oil in step 2, the grains become fluffy and well separated when steamed. This rice is equally delicious with grilled, broiled, or baked meat, fish or poultry.

TZATZIKI

4 large cloves garlic	1 quart plain yogurt
Pinch of salt	¼ cup olive oil
½ to 1 whole cucumber, washed and dried	¼ cup red wine vinegar

1. Mash the garlic cloves with the flat of a large knife or cleaver. Add the salt and continue to mash until a fine paste is formed.
2. Grate the unpeeled cucumber. Combine in a bowl with the yogurt, mashed garlic, oil, and vinegar. Mix thoroughly. Taste; if there is no pronounced garlic flavor, mash and add more.
3. Let sit for several hours at room temperature or overnight in the refrigerator.

This is a typical Greek hors d'oeuvre. It is also delicious, however, as an accompaniment to lamb or beef.

GALAKTOBOUREKO

1 pound fillo leaves, at room temperature	SYRUP
½ pound butter, melted	Cinnamon (optional)
CUSTARD	Sliced orange (optional)

Method 1 (Pan-Style):

1. Preheat oven to 350°.
2. Layer 4 sheets of fillo, each lightly but completely buttered on one side, in a loaf pan in such a way that enough of an overhang is left all the way around to fold over the top of the Custard. Be sure that the leaves overlap adequately to seal the Custard within them.
3. Spread the Custard evenly within the fillo leaves. Fold the overhanging leaves to cover.
4. Layer 3 to 5 more lightly but evenly buttered fillo leaves over. Top with an unbuttered leaf. Fold the edges and corners neatly.
5. With a sharp knife, cut diagonally through only the two top layers of fillo to mark diamond-shaped portions. Butter the top layer of fillo.
6. Bake in preheated oven for approximately 45 minutes, or until the fillo is puffed and golden brown. (Begin checking at 30 minutes if you suspect your oven to operate hot.) Remove and pour the cooled Syrup over the surface. Allow to cool for at least 1 hour or until set before cutting into portions.

If using this traditional method of preparation, the custard may be slightly warm to start.

Method 2 (Floyeres):

1. Preheat oven to 350°.
2. Layer 2 fillo leaves, each lightly but evenly buttered on one side, on a working surface. Center ½ cup (or an ice-cream scoop) of the Custard on the nearest end of the top leaf. Fold both sides of the fillo toward the center, partially covering the custard. Starting at the end with the custard, roll up like an egg roll. Place seam side down in a deep pan. Butter the top and ends.
3. Repeat until all the Custard is used, placing 1 inch apart in the pan.
4. Bake in preheated oven for 30 minutes or until puffed and golden brown, beginning to check at 20 minutes. Remove from the oven and pour the cooled Syrup over. Serve immediately or allow to cool;

pour additional syrup from the pan over the rolls at serving time. Lightly sprinkle with cinnamon and top each with a thin slice of orange.

To manage the rolling of the Floyeres, or flutes, you must be sure the custard is thoroughly cooled and thickened beforehand. The name for this method of preparation derives from the similarity to the reed flutes of the Greek shepherds.

CUSTARD

6 cups whole milk	5 eggs
1⅔ cups sugar	Peel of ½ lemon,
½ cup plus 1 tablespoon	finely grated
Cream of Wheat	1 teaspoon vanilla extract

1. Place the milk and half the sugar in a saucepan. Bring to a boil, stirring frequently.
2. In a mixing bowl large enough to hold all the ingredients, place the remaining sugar, the Cream of Wheat, and eggs. Whisk for 2 to 3 minutes.
3. As soon as the milk reaches a boil, whisk gradually into the egg mixture, stirring constantly. Continue to stir—vigorously at first, more slowly toward the end, and being sure to reach to the bottom of the bowl—until all ingredients are well combined.
4. Add the grated lemon peel and vanilla extract and continue to whisk for 3 to 4 minutes. The mixture will begin to thicken slightly, and barely begin to bubble, around the edges. At this point, stop beating—it will curdle if overbeaten. Allow to cool before using.

It is ideal to make the custard in the morning, or even the day ahead, especially if using the second method of preparation.

SYRUP

2 cups sugar	1 stick cinnamon
Juice of 1 lemon	

1. Place the ingredients with 1 cup water in a small saucepan. Bring to a boil and cook for 1 minute. Remove from heat and allow to cool.

CRÊPE de PARIS

Dinner for Six

*Feuilleté aux Pointes Asperges avec des Huîtres
à la Vapeur de Cresson*

Salade Insolite

Filet d'Halibut au Fenouil et au Pernod

Fraises au Coulis de Framboises

Wine:

*With Appetizer and Salad—St. Véran, Villamont,
or
Entre-Deux-Mers*

With Entrée—a rich white Burgundy (1976 is great)

With Dessert—Champagne or Hugel Gewürztraminer Réserve

Annie Agostini, Owner

CRÊPE DE PARIS

T he sophisticated, airy feeling of the Crêpe de Paris in Rainier Square is a far cry from the humble beginnings, however quaint and charming, of the original restaurant which Annie Agostini opened in 1968. The Rainier Square location has parquet wood floors, imported area rugs, chrome and leather chairs, contemporary wood tables with fresh daisy centerpieces and huge potted palms everywhere. Everything is set against white: white walls, some with free-formed shapes, and a white ceiling, banded in geometric tiers for a stunning effect. And the restaurant is not just a crêpery. It has evolved into one of the best places in the city to find truly creative French food.

There are four different menus at Crêpe de Paris. The luncheon menu includes specialties, salads, sandwiches and a cold buffet, as well as the large variety of crêpes. The dinner menu is constantly changing. Annie calls her suppliers each morning to see what is the best of the available fresh produce and fish, and her menu for the day reflects her selections. "I am very proud of the menu. I work very hard to research and find new ideas, to use the freshest and finest ingredients."On the dinner menu, each sauce for each person is prepared individually and at the last minute. "It is the only way to achieve top quality." After the dinner, a dessert menu is presented which includes "Les Specialties," dessert wines, in addition to the fifteen varieties of sweet crêpes. The last of the four food menus is a lighter, late evening menu featuring soups, salads, dinner and dessert crêpes, and other dessert specialities. A wine list of over 60 wines and a captain's list of wines are also available.

Crêpe de Paris has a private dining room that seats up to 12 comfortably for luncheon or dinner events. The restaurant can accommodate 120 diners at a sit down meal, and up to 300 for cocktails and hors d'oeuvres. In the summers there is a lovely outside terrace, where there have been parties and wedding receptions of 500 guests.

The success of Crêpe de Paris is no accident. Perhaps Annie sums it up best by her attitude: "We want people who come here to have a beautiful time and the best possible food. To do this, I must use energy and imagination. I put my whole self into it."

Rainier Square
1333 5th Avenue North

FEUILLETÉ AUX POINTES ASPERGES AVEC DES HUÎTRES Á LA VAPEUR DE CRESSON

36 small, fresh green
    asparagus tips
24 oysters, opened, out
    of shell
½ bunch watercress
1½ cups white wine
⅔ pint whipping cream
½ to ¾ cup SAUCE VIN BLANC

½ can green asparagus,
    puréed
Juice of ½ lemon
1 teaspoon Cognac
1 cube butter
Salt and pepper to taste
6 FEUILLETÉ

1. Rapidly poach asparagus in boiling salted water until cooked but firm.

2. Put the asparagus into a saucepan with the oysters and 4 watercress leaves. Add the white wine. Cover. Let boil slowly for 10 seconds, then remove the asparagus and oysters.

3. Reduce the wine until the consistency of a syrup. Add the cream. Reduce the mixture again.

4. Add the Sauce Vin Blanc, 1 teaspoon asparagus purée, lemon juice and Cognac. Turn off the heat when the desired consistency is achieved.

5. While stirring gently, add the butter in small pieces until well incorporated. Correct the seasoning with salt and pepper. Place asparagus and oysters into sauce to warm.

6. Arrange the asparagus and oysters on the lower halves of Feuilleté. Cover with sauce. Place the top on the Feuilleté. Decorate with a few leaves of watercress.

SAUCE VIN BLANC

2 large onions, minced
1 leek, white part only,
    minced
2 tablespoons butter
2 to 3 pounds clean halibut or
    sole bones
½ cup white wine
    Few parsley stems,
    cleaned

Few mushroom stems,
    cleaned
Bouquet garni (½ bay
    leaf, ¼ teaspoon thyme)
½ to ⅔ cup whipping cream
    Beurre manié

1. Mince the onions and white of the leek. Simmer slowly the onions and leek with the butter in a large covered stock pot for 5 to 10 minutes. Add the fish bones, which have been washed in cold, running water for 1 to 2 hours to take out all the blood parts. Break the bones with a wooden spoon. Add the wine, parsley stems, mushroom stems and bouquet garni. Cover with water and bring to a boil. Skim, and let cook slowly for 20 to 25 minutes. Pass the fumet through a thin china cup or cheesecloth. Be sure to muddle as well as possible to obtain all the flavor from the bones. Makes about 3 quarts of stock.

2. Place the fumet into a thick pot. Bring to a boil and then reduce the fumet completely by evaporation until a dark, thick, syrup-like mixture is obtained. Add the cream and reduce again. While the cream and fumet are reducing, be certain that the edges of the pot do not get a reddish build-up that will ruin the color and taste of the sauce. Whip frequently. When the mixture is like a smooth sauce, turn off the heat and add the beurre manié, made of 1½ teaspoons flour mixed well with 1 teaspoon soft butter. Whip until well blended.

3. Return to heat and cook sauce for 10 to 15 minutes, very slowly. Add a bit of wine and cream to keep the consistency appropriate. Pass the sauce through a very fine strainer or a cheese cloth. Reserve.

CRÊPE DE PARIS

PÂTE FEUILLETÉ

1 pound pastry flour
6 tablespoons soft butter
Pinch salt
¾ to 1 cup water

1 pound cold butter
1 egg yolk mixed with a bit
of water ("egg wash" or
dorure)

1. Place the flour, soft butter, salt and water into a food processor with a plastic blade. Process for 15 to 20 seconds. Remove the dough and place in plastic in the refrigerator for 2 hours, or overnight.

2. Place the dough on a lightly floured table or board and make a square of 10 to 15 inches. The dough should not be rolled thinner than ¼ inch.

3. Remove the pound of butter from the refrigerator and put it into a plastic bag. Pound it with a rolling pin until it forms an 8-inch square (½ inch thick).

4. Place the butter on the center of the dough, making a perpendicular losange (diamond). Fold each corner of the dough over the butter. Turn the dough over, flour the table, and roll the dough into a rectangle of about 16 or 18 inches in length, keeping the width quite narrow.

5. Fold the dough into three parts, like a letter. Turn it a quarter of a turn, and roll it again into a 16- to 18-inch length. Fold it once again in the same way. Put the dough into a plastic bag in the refrigerator for 20 minutes. This completes two turns.

6. Do two more turns; place the dough back into the refrigerator for another 20 minutes.

7. Do two more turns, making six turns altogether; place the dough back into the refrigerator for 20 minutes.

8. Preheat oven to 425°.

9. Roll the chilled Pâte Feuilleté until it is uniformly ¼ inch thick.

10. Cut 12 rectangles of about 3½ by 2 inches. Place six of them on a sheet pan. Very lightly wash them with the dorure.

11. Arrange the remaining 6 rectangles on top of the first ones. Wash with dorure again.

12. Bake for 15 to 20 minutes in preheated oven until lightly golden brown. Do not open the oven door or they will fall. If there is no glass in the door, very gently open the door after 15 minutes, and take a quick peek. When they are ready, remove from the oven, let cool for a few minutes, and then split the tops.

SALADE INSOLITE

2 *hearts of Bibb lettuce*	2 *tablespoons oil*
2 *hearts of romaine*	*Salt and pepper*
½ *carrot, julienned*	⅓ *cup good red wine vinegar*
1 *stalk celery, julienned*	*DRESSING DE BASE*
1 *bunch watercress*	18 *small slices of smoked*
9 *chicken livers, cleaned*	*salmon, rolled (3 to*
and halved	*4 ounces)*

1. Clean lettuce and romaine. Be careful not to cut the leaves. Pat dry.

2. Arrange the Bibb lettuce in the centers of 7-inch salad plates, forming a little dome. Place the julienned carrots, celery and watercress on the lettuce. Arrange 3 small romaine leaves evenly around the dome. Refrigerate.

3. In a sauté pan, sauté chicken livers in hot oil for a few minutes on each side. Add salt and pepper to taste. Deglaze the pan with vinegar. Let the vinegar cook down for a few minutes until it is foamy and syrupy. Turn the heat off. Add Dressing De Base, mixing in evenly.

4. Arrange 3 pieces of liver on each plate around the lettuce, forming a triangle. Place the smoked salmon between each piece of liver. Top with warm dressing. Serve immediately.

DRESSING DE BASE

1 egg yolk
1 teaspoon Dijon mustard
½ pint pure vegetable oil
½ pint olive oil
   Juice of ½ lemon

2 tablespoons red wine
   vinegar
   Salt and freshly ground
   pepper

1. Place egg yolk and mustard in a small bowl. Whip for a few seconds and then add the vegetable oil very slowly, continuing to whip.

2. Add the olive oil in the same way. Slowly add lemon juice and vinegar. Salt and pepper to taste. Set aside.

FILET D'HALIBUT AU FENOUIL ET AU PERNOD

1 stalk fennel
6 fresh halibut steaks, 6 to
   8 ounces each
   Salt and pepper
   Lemon juice
   Flour
¼ cup vegetable oil
¾ cup white wine
1 pint whipping cream

1 cup SAUCE VIN
   BLANC (see page 50)
   Juice of 1 lemon
1 tablespoon Pernod
6 tablespoons cold butter,
   cut into small chunks
   Watercress, for decoration

1. Preheat oven to 375°.

2. Wash the fennel; cut into fourths and then mince. Poach in boiling water for a few minutes to blanch, then cool it down with cold water. Strain and reserve.

3. Season halibut steaks with salt, pepper and a little lemon juice. Flour the steaks lightly. Arrange them in a large sauté pan in which the oil has been placed. Get the pan very hot, then turn the fish over and finish cooking in the oven for 8 to 12 minutes. The halibut is ready when it is firm in the center. Do not overcook. Fish is best when very

juicy. It can be slightly under-cooked, so that it can continue to cook while waiting for the sauce. When the fish is ready, place on a plate and keep in a warm place.

4. Deglaze the pan by adding the blanched fennel and the white wine. Reduce the mixture until it is like a syrup. Add ⅔ of the cream; reduce again until there is a nice consistency.

5. Add the Sauce Vin Blanc, lemon juice and Pernod. Correct the seasoning to taste. Turn off the heat when the right consistency is obtained. Add a little more cream if desired. Add the cold butter, whipping gently until very smooth. Correct the seasoning once again.

6. Place one halibut steak on each plate. Spoon the sauce over. Decorate with watercress.

FRAISES AU COULIS DE FRAMBOISES

*6 to 8 large strawberries per
      person
½ pound frozen raspberries,
      well drained of liquid
      (use fresh raspberries
      when available)*

*½ cup sugar
1 tablespoon Kirschwasser
      Juice of ½ lemon
6 mint leaves*

1. Wash the strawberries quickly. Stem them with a paring knife.

2. Prepare the coulis (sauce) by placing the raspberries, sugar, Kirschwasser and lemon juice into a food processor. Process for 10 seconds.

3. Strain the coulis through a small china cup or through a cloth to eliminate seeds.

4. Arrange the strawberries grouped together in the center on individual plates. Top strawberries with coulis and garnish with mint leaves.

Dinner for Four

French Onion Soup

Shrimp and Butter Lettuce Salad

Stir-Fry Vegetables and Prawns

Herbed and Wild Rice

Chocolate Mousse Pie

Wine:

Puligny-Montrachet

Bill & John Schwarz, Owners

Gary Rowe, Manager

Andy Graham, Assistant Manager

DANIEL'S BROILER

V ivid, multi-colored sails on boats almost near enough to touch, a breathtaking view of Mount Rainier on a clear night, and the joy of watching a full moon rise over Bellevue: all this and more comes with the dinner at Daniel's Broiler. From every seat in the dining room, one can observe the majesty of Lake Washington, for Daniel's Broiler virtually sits on the shores of the lake, and many of the dinner patrons arrive by boat. The setting is the YABA Yacht Basin at Leschi, in the space that once housed the picturesque Seaborn's Marina. Now the floor-to-ceiling wood-frame windows, designed in a stunning geometric pattern, enclose the elegant, comfortable, contemporary retreat where dinner is served nightly.

The restaurant first opened in January, 1980, but its owner Dan Sandal sold it a year later to the Butcher Organization, an association of restaurants headed by the Schwartz brothers, Bill and John. The organization embraces Henry's Off Broadway, two Butcher Restaurants, three Benjamin's Restaurants, and three Sandwich Shop & Pie Places. Daniel's is the smallest of the dinner restaurants and a unique compliment to its siblings. John Schwartz explains: "We are more than a steak house; we have become a specialized broiler. Our emphasis now is on seafood because our customers have dictated their preference. Probably 70 to 80 percent of the dinners we serve are seafood, and most are broiled right in full view of the customer."

"We serve fairly simple food," adds Gary Rowe, "but we use the best ingredients possible." The patron's wishes are considered foremost. "We are a customer-oriented restaurant; if someone requests a special sauce or a certain seasoning and we have the ingredients in our kitchen, we will prepare it gladly."

From the 96 candle-like lights on the extraordinary copper chandelier which encompasses the entire ceiling of the restaurant, to the constantly changing view from the windows, Daniel's Broiler is a comfortably elegant, predictably delicious place to dine.

200 Lake Washington Boulevard

FRENCH ONION SOUP

4 tablespoons butter	3 tablespoons olive oil (approximately)
4 onions, cut in ¼" julienne	8 thin slices French baguette loaf
2 cloves garlic, minced	½ pound Gruyère cheese, shredded
¼ cup flour	2 teaspoons chopped fresh parsley
5⅓ cups BROWN STOCK or beef broth	
⅓ cup Chablis	
¼ teaspoon coarsely ground pepper	

1. Preheat oven to 350°.
2. Melt the butter in a sauté pan over medium-high heat. Add the onions and 1 minced clove of garlic; sauté until the onions are lightly browned.
3. Spread the flour over the surface of a baking pan and bake in preheated oven until lightly browned. Add to the onions and mix well.
4. Place the Brown Stock in a large pot. Stir in the onion mixture, wine, and pepper. Bring to a boil, reduce heat, and simmer 1 hour, skimming the surface every 15 minutes.
5. Sauté the remaining garlic in about 3 tablespoons olive oil until it begins to brown. Remove the garlic and discard; brown the sliced bread well in the seasoned oil.
6. A few minutes before serving, preheat the broiler. Ladle the soup into individual heated crocks.Top each serving with two of the croutons and one-fourth of the shredded cheese. Place under the broiler until the cheese is melted and very lightly browned. Garnish each with a sprinkle of chopped parsley and serve.

BROWN STOCK

2½ pounds beef or veal bones or trimmings (or a combination)
½ onion, diced large
1 stalk celery, diced large
1 carrot, sliced in large chunks
1 bay leaf
1 clove garlic, halved
Pinch of thyme
1 cup red wine
1 cup white wine
3 to 4 whole peppercorns
Salt

1. Break the bones with a heavy cleaver. Place the bones and trimmings in a roasting pan and bake at 300° for 1 hour or until the bones are well browned.
2. Add the vegetables, bay leaf, and garlic. Bake until all are tender, about 30 minutes.
3. Add the thyme and red and white wines; deglaze the pan over high heat. Transfer everything to a large stock pot.
4. Add 3 quarts water and the peppercorns and bring to a boil. Cook until reduced by half, skimming frequently.
5. Strain through a china cap, discarding all solid matter. Return to heat, skimming until clear.
6. Pass through a fine-mesh sieve. Add salt to taste.

SHRIMP AND BUTTER LETTUCE SALAD

2 heads butter lettuce
1 cup DRESSING
1 hard-cooked egg, shredded
½ pound baby shrimp
1 tomato, sliced in eighths
½ cup croutons

1. Wash lettuce heads well and let dry overnight, inverted on a towel in the refrigerator.
2. When ready to serve, cut or tear the lettuce into 1- to 2-inch pieces into a large mixing bowl. Pour the Dressing over the lettuce and toss lightly until well covered.
3. Portion the salad onto four individual salad plates. Top with the shredded hard-cooked egg, baby shrimp, diced tomato, and croutons.

DRESSING

2 teaspoons tarragon vinegar
Juice of 1 medium-size
  lemon
¼ teaspoon oregano
¼ teaspoon basil

1 egg, coddled 1½ minutes
¼ teaspoon Dijon mustard
¼ teaspoon garlic salt
¾ cup olive oil
Salt and pepper to taste

1. Whip together all ingredients except the olive oil, salt, and pepper in a small mixing bowl.
2. Slowly add the olive oil in a stream, whipping continuously with a wire whisk by hand or on low speed with an electric mixer until the dressing is of a creamy consistency. Finish by adding salt and pepper to taste.

STIR-FRY VEGETABLES AND PRAWNS

½ cup coconut oil
24 (16- to 20-count) prawns,
  cleaned
1 tablespoon seasoning salt
1 tablespoon finely minced
  fresh ginger
1 clove fresh garlic,
  minced
1 carrot, cut in julienne
2 stalks celery, sliced
  on the diagonal
¼ pound fresh pea pods

½ onion, thinly sliced
¼ pound mushrooms,
  thinly sliced
Juice of 2 lemons
¼ cup vermouth
2 tomatoes, halved and
  thinly sliced
¼ cup teriyaki sauce
4 teaspoons toasted sesame
  seeds
¼ cup chopped green onion
Lemon wedges

1. Add the coconut oil to a sauté pan or wok and place over medium-high heat until the oil is hot. Add the prawns and season with approximately ¾ teaspoon of the seasoning salt. Cook, stirring constantly, until the prawns begin to curl slightly.
2. Stir in the ginger and garlic; sauté for 30 seconds.

3. Stir in the carrot, celery, pea pods, and onion, seasoning lightly again with approximately ½ teaspoon seasoning salt. Sauté for approximately 1 minute.

4. Stir in the sliced mushrooms and the remaining seasoning salt; sauté 1 minute.

5. Add the lemon juice, vermouth, and tomatoes continuing to sauté for 1 minute longer.

6. Pour in the teriyake sauce and toss lightly. Turn the mixture out onto a platter, then top with the toasted sesame seeds and green onion. Garnish with lemon wedges around the edge of the platter. Serve immediately.

I like this recipe because it is so quick, so simple to prepare, and yet such an interesting interplay of flavors.

HERBED AND WILD RICE

4 tablespoons clarified butter

3 tablespoons finely diced onion

2 tablespoons sliced mushrooms

Pinch of thyme

Pinch of sage

3 ounces wild rice, well washed

2 cups CHICKEN STOCK (see page 6)

⅓ cup white rice, well washed

2 tablespoons vermicelli, broken into ¼" pieces

1 small clove garlic, grated

1 teaspoon diced red pepper

1. Heat 3 tablespoons clarified butter in a medium saucepan. Add 1 tablespoon of the onion and the mushrooms and sauté until the onion is soft. Add the thyme and sage; reduce heat and simmer for 5 minutes.

2. Add the wild rice and 1⅓ cups of the chicken stock. Bring to a boil, reduce heat, and simmer 1 hour.

3. Separately, sauté the remaining onion in the remaining clarified butter. When transparent, add the broken vermicelli and white rice. Sauté until lightly browned, stirring constantly and being careful not to burn.

4. Add the grated garlic and sauté for 1 minute more.

5. Add the remaining ⅔ cup chicken stock and bring to a boil. Immediately upon reaching a boil, cover and reduce heat to simmer. Cook 20 minutes without lifting the cover.

6. Stir with a fork, remove from heat, and let stand 5 minutes.

7. Drain off any liquid remaining in the wild rice pan. Allow to cool slightly, then combine with the white rice and diced red pepper. Reheat in a warm oven until ready to serve.

CHOCOLATE MOUSSE PIE

1½ pounds French vanilla chocolate (preferably Guittard)	6 egg yolks, lightly beaten
1 cup butter	2 tablespoons Grand Marnier liqueur
1½ cups whipping cream	2 tablespoons ground walnuts
10 egg whites	CRUST

1. Melt the chocolate and butter in the top of a double boiler over medium heat. When melted, stir to blend and set aside to cool. Continue with the preparation only when the chocolate mixture has cooled to slightly above room temperature.

2. Whip the cream until stiff, then set aside. Whip the egg whites until stiff but not dry. Fold the egg whites into the whipped cream.

3. Add the lightly beaten egg yolks to the cooled chocolate mixture; mix well.

4. Gently fold the chocolate mixture into the egg whites and whipped cream. Fold in the Grand Marnier and ground walnuts. Continue folding until the mousse has an even consistency.

5. Spoon the mousse onto the crust and spread evenly in the pan. Shake the pan to remove any air pockets. Chill the pie in the refrigerator for 2 to 4 hours before serving.

DANIEL'S BROILER

CRUST

1 cup graham cracker
  crumbs
3 tablespoons ground
  walnuts

2 tablespoons sugar
¼ teaspoon cinnamon
¼ teaspoon nutmeg
¼ cup butter

Mix all ingredients thoroughly and press firmly into the bottom of a 9-inch springform pan.

Eating this dessert is almost gluttonous, because it is so rich. It is a truly hedonistic delight.

Dinner for Four

Cheeseboard

Tempura Vegetables with Dips

Caesar Salad

Nova Scotia Scallops

Rack of Lamb

Pier Pie

Wine:

With Cheeseboard and Tempura—Wehlener Sonnenuhr Kabinett, 1978

With Salad and Scallops—Clos du Val Chardonnay, 1978

*With Lamb—Beaulieu Vineyards Cabernet Sauvignon
Private Reserve, 1974*

With Dessert—Sandeman Port

Duke Moscrip, Owner

Jack Jones, Head Chef

The fact that Duke Moscrip was once a star basketball player may have something to do with the reputation of Duke's as a hang-out for local sports celebrities; but the comfortable, unique ambiance—a clubby, semi-elegant neighborhood hang-out—was most assuredly created for more than the athlete.

After six years as a stockbroker, Duke was initially attracted to the restaurant business as a good investment. It was his personal desire to "have a place I could go to, to be a hang-out, to get real American-type food" that inspired him. "I woke up one morning and the restaurant was all laid out in front of me."

"I got tired of going to restaurants that required people to act a certain way. Duke's is a renegade restaurant. It disdains pretention, tradition and inflexibility; it was the first one of this calibre to do that."

"Duke's is unique because it allows people freedom to be what they want to be that night—not on stage." It is clearly unstructured and accommodating for the customer, who is not burdened with a lot of rules and regulations regarding split orders, minimum charges, or eating dinner in the bar. Sampling different appetizers, combining half orders of dinners, or trying several varieties of wine by the glass are encouraged. Duke's bar is known as an "in" spot on lower Queen Anne Hill, with its flair for the contemporary and the unique variety in both the wine list and drinks.

The quality of Queen Anne Duke's is mirrored in its sibling restaurants. The Bellevue Duke's is now five years old, and is a varitable twin of the original in menu, decor, and personality. The third Duke's, a bit more up-scale in atmosphere but still preserving the great food and prices, opened in February, 1985, near the Fifth Avenue Theater.

"The restaurant is very sly; it's not what it appears to be sometimes. For some it appears to be a bar with food as a sidelight. It's not, because in addition we have fresh seafood, aged meat, homemade pies, and fresh squeezed juices—high quality food and the best of everything." For others, however, the continually changing "special board" is the main attraction, offering intriguing new items daily. Yet for just about everyone, it's hard not to want to "belong" to Duke's. The loyalty of the regular customers clearly reflects that.

236 1st Avenue West

CHEESEBOARD

4 ounces New York Sharp Cheddar cheese	1 Granny Smith apple, or other firm, tart variety
4 ounces Jarlsberg cheese	Fresh strawberries or sliced melon
4 ounces Brie cheese	Dates
2 ounces Gjetost (goat's cheese)	Hot sourdough bread
2 ounces bleu cheese, crumbled	

1. Slice the Cheddar, Jarlsberg and Gjetost. Arrange on wooden cheeseboard by fanning out. Place Brie and bleu cheese on board and garnish with fruits and dates.

2. Serve with hot sourdough bread.

This item epitomizes the restaurant's approach to food. It can be a casual snack, but it's healthy, different, and can make a substantial meal with a good bottle of wine.

All cheeses will taste best if served at room temperature.

TEMPURA VEGETABLES WITH DIPS

8 medium mushrooms	Peanut oil
1 zucchini	TEMPURA BATTER
1 carrot	SOUR CREAM DIP
1 green pepper	SOY DIP
4 to 8 asparagus spears	

1. Scrub mushrooms. Wash all other vegetables. Allow to dry thoroughly. Cut zucchini and carrots in half; then slice lengthwise into ½-inch wide strips. Take seeds out of inside of green pepper and cut into strips.

2. Pour the peanut oil into a heavy skillet to a depth of about 1½ inches. Make sure the oil is very hot.

3. Dip the vegetables one at a time in the batter and then place in the oil. As they are frying together, make sure they do not stick together and be careful not to overcook. Fry to a light golden brown. Place on paper towels and drain off excess oil.

4. Serve on platter with the two dips in the center.

TEMPURA BATTER

5 eggs	1 teaspoon Worcestershire
1½ cups water	sauce
1 tablespoon salt	3¼ cups cake flour

Mix ingredients together in large bowl until well blended.

SOUR CREAM DIP

Mix 3 parts sour cream to 1 part Dijon mustard.

SOY DIP

½ cup soy sauce	2 tablespoons sherry
¼ teaspoon powdered ginger	1 tablespoon lime juice

Mix together, preferably ahead of time so flavors can blend.

CAESAR SALAD

1 head romaine lettuce	2 ounces grated Parmesan
1 egg	cheese
5 ounces olive oil	Salt
10 drops Worcester-	Pepper
shire sauce	½ cup croutons
Juice of 1 lemon	

1. Wash romaine leaves and pat dry. Break off 10 to 12 whole leaves.
2. Break egg into large mixing bowl. Whip with wire whisk while adding the olive oil. Continue whipping and add the Worchestershire sauce and lemon juice. Sprinkle in 1 ounce of the Parmesan cheese. Season with salt and pepper.
3. Brush each romaine leaf through the dressing and coat both sides. Arrange and overlap leaves in a large salad bowl and top with croutons which have been mixed with the remaining dressing.
4. Sprinkle 1 ounce more of Paremsan over top of salad. Serve with hot damp hand towels rolled up.

It is said that this is the original Caesar salad recipe from Caesar Cardini's restaurant in Tijuana. It is meant to be eaten with one's fingers, usually by rolling up each leaf.

NOVA SCOTIA SCALLOPS

16 ounces frozen Nova Scotia	2 teaspoons butter
sea scallops	Salt
½ to 1 cup flour	Pepper
2 ounces olive oil	1 lemon, cut into wedges
¼ teaspoon minced garlic	Parsley, chopped

1. Thaw scallops. Roll in flour and shake off excess.
2. In coated teflon fry pan, place the olive oil and heat over a high flame. Drop the scallops in a single layer. Reduce heat to medium.

3. When bottom side is a golden brown, turn once and add the garlic. Continue cooking until scallops are completely browned. Remove from heat and pour off oil. Add the butter and season with salt and pepper. Roll scallops in pan until butter is melted.

4. Serve garnished with a lemon wedge and parsley lightly sprinkled over the top.

Use a teflon pan and disturb the scallops in pan as little as possible so as not to separate the breading from the scallops.

These should have a very light breading. A straightforward, clean presentation for scallops.

RACK OF LAMB

2 imported New Zealand racks of lamb (approximately 16 ribs)	*MARINADE* *Sour cream* *Mint jelly*

1. Mix together ingredients for Marinade in a saucepan and bring to a boil. Cool.

2. Have your butcher remove the chine bone from the racks upon purchasing. With a very sharp knife, separate ribs by cutting half way through the meat. Remove the fat cap off the back side of the rack. Marinate racks overnight.

3. When ready to serve, broil the racks on all possible sides until done, approximately 8 to 10 minutes for medium rare.

4. Serve each rack with a little each of sour cream and mint jelly on the side.

Do not try to cut the rack until it is completely thawed out.

MARINADE

1½ cups apple juice
2 garlic cloves, crushed
1 orange, sliced

½ cup soy sauce
Juice of 1 lemon

PIER PIE

1 cup homemade chocolate
   chips, crumbled
1 cup graham cracker
   crumbs
¼ cup sugar
1 cube butter, melted
   Hot fudge topping, room
   temperature

1 quart coffee (or mocha)
   ice cream
1 quart chocolate ice cream
   Approximately ¼ cup
   roasted slivered almonds
   Freshly whipped cream

1. Mix together first four ingredients and press into a 10-inch pie plate which has been brushed with butter. Bake 7 minutes at 350°. Chill in freezer until firm.
2. Spread fudge topping over crust to form a layer about ¼ inch thick. Refreeze.
3. Let the coffee ice cream soften slightly to a spreadable consistency but do not let it totally melt. Smooth over crust. Refreeze until solid.
4. Repeat with the chocolate ice cream. Top with almonds. Freeze for 3 more hours. At serving time, top with freshly whipped cream.

Do not try to substitute a chocolate "syrup" for the fudge topping.

This recipe was named after, and borrowed from, the Pier Restaurant in Newport, Rhode Island.

Dinner for Six

Foie Gras Salad with Turnips and Spinach

Vineyard Snails with White Wine, Grapes, and Chanterelles

Medallions of Veal with Orange and Lemon

Terrine of White Wine

Wine:

With Snails—Chateau St. Jean Fumé Blanc, 1980

With Veal—Château Pontet-Canet, Haut-Médoc, 1976

Four Seasons Hotels, Owner

THE GEORGIAN ROOM AT THE FOUR SEASONS

When the Olympic Hotel first opened in 1924, it was hailed as the grandest hotel west of Chicago. Surrounding the old Metropolitan Theater on three sides, the Olympic was built at a cost of 5.5 million dollars by a community of 4,500 Seattle investors on the site of what was once the first building of the University of Washington.

In 1861, Arthur A. Denny, Charles Terry, and Edward Landert, Seattle pioneers, donated ten acres of beautiful land overlooking Elliott Bay to the Territory of Washington to be used for a university site. When the University of Washington moved to northeast Seattle in 1895, it retained ownership of the downtown property which housed its first buildings. To this day, the University owns the land and the Olympic Hotel building, which has been declared an historic monument and is listed on the National Register of Historic Places. In 1980, the Four Seasons Hotels and the Urban Investment and Development Company signed a 60-year lease with the University, and today, after renovation and restoration, the hotel is known as the Four Seasons Olympic.

The Georgian was the main dining room of the original Olympic, as it is in today's Four Seasons Hotel. The room has magnificent two-story palladian windows which were blacked out during the Second World War and not restored until the 1980's to once again allow light into the spacious room. Its softly colored fabrics and rich marble accents make the Georgian warm and comfortable.

The menu has been structured to make the Georgian a restaurant for all occasions: a simple and relaxing evening meal, a grand business entertainment, or a very special event. All in all, the main emphasis of the Georgian is to offer a variety of Northwest favorites with friendly and efficient service which make each and every guest feel at complete ease.

The Four Seasons Olympic has a precious history. Six United States Presidents, leaders and princes of many nations have been guests of the hotel. Its ballrooms and restaurants have witnessed the special occasions of Seattle for over half a century.

411 University Street

FOIE GRAS SALAD WITH TURNIPS AND SPINACH

18 ounces foie gras
(goose liver)
6 ounces turnips

2 bunches fresh spinach
OIL AND VINEGAR
DRESSING

1. Melt a little butter in a sauté pan over moderately high heat. Add the foie gras and sauté until half-done (pink inside), about 4 to 5 minutes. Remove from heat.
2. Cut the turnips in very fine julienne strips. Blanch for 1 minute in boiling water and drain immediately.
3. Wash the spinach thoroughly and dry well. Remove the stems.
4. Combine the julienned turnip and the spinach. Toss with Oil and Vinegar Dressing. Arrange on individual salad plates.
5. Cut the foie gras in julienne sticks, about 1½ inches by ¼ inch by ⅛ inch, or in ¼-inch cubes. Sprinkle over the salads.

OIL AND VINEGAR DRESSING

1 teaspoon finely chopped
shallot
½ teaspoon Dijon mustard
Salt and pepper to taste

2 dashes Worcestershire
sauce
½ cup red wine vinegar
¾ cup olive oil

1. Combine the shallots, mustard, salt, pepper, Worcestershire sauce, and 2 tablespoons of the vinegar, mixing well.
2. Add the olive oil gradually, blending with a whisk.
3. Add the remaining vinegar, whisking thoroughly.

VINEYARD SNAILS WITH WHITE WINE, GRAPES, AND CHANTERELLES

½ pound chanterelle
   mushrooms
¼ pound butter
36 escargots
1 pound white grapes,
   peeled
½ teaspoon flour

1 cup Riesling wine
2 tablespoons cream
   Salt and pepper to taste
3 drops Worcestershire
   sauce
   Pinch of nutmeg

1. Sauté the chanterelles in 4 tablespoons of the butter for 2 minutes. Remove from the pan with a slotted spoon and set aside.
2. In a separate pan, sauté the snails for 3 to 4 minutes with the remaining 4 tablespoons butter.
3. Add the peeled grapes and sauté for 1 minute more. Add the flour and stir until the butter and flour have blended. Add the chanterelles and the wine and bring to a boil, stirring constantly.
4. When the sauce has thickened slightly, add the cream and return to a boil. Remove from heat.
5. Season with salt, pepper, Worcestershire sauce, and nutmeg.

The key to this recipe is to make the sauce very light and not too thick.

MEDALLIONS OF VEAL WITH ORANGE AND LEMON

3 *pounds red potatoes*	*Pepper to taste*
½ *pound butter*	*Juice and zest of 1*
Salt to taste	*small orange*
2 *pounds snow peas*	*Juice and zest of 2*
12 *(4-ounce) slices veal loin*	*medium lemons*
Flour	

1. Peel the potatoes, and cut into ¼-inch cubes.
2. In ¼ pound butter, sauté the potatoes until golden brown on all sides and cooked. Season with salt and set aside.
3. Snap off the ends of the snow peas and remove the strings. Blanch in salted water for 6 to 8 minutes; drain and set aside.
4. Dust the veal slices lightly with flour. Season with salt and pepper to taste. Sauté in ¼ pound butter for approximately 3 minutes on each side, being careful not to overcook.
5. When the veal is cooked, add the juices of the orange and lemons to the pan and bring to a quick boil.
6. Remove the meat from the pan and arrange on dinner plates.
7. Cook the pan juices to reduce by about half. Add the orange and lemon zest.
8. Spoon the sauce over the meat. Arrange the potatoes and the snow peas on the plates and serve.

TERRINE OF WHITE WINE

6 *egg yolks*	3½ *leaves gelatin (optional)*
5 *tablespoons sugar*	1 *pint whipping cream,*
1 *cup white wine*	*whipped*

1. Mix the egg yolks and sugar until creamy.
2. Bring the wine to a boil; reduce heat to low and add the sugar/egg mixture. Maintain on low heat, but do not allow to boil, for 3 minutes, stirring constantly. Remove from heat.
3. If using the gelatin, soften in warm water and stir into the egg mixture.
4. Fold in the whipped cream. If gelatin is used, pour into individual molds; otherwise, pour into large wine glasses. Refrigerate at least 1 hour before serving.

Note: The gelatin, if used, produces a more firmly textured terrine. To unmold, set the molds in hot water for 30 seconds, then turn out onto dessert plates.

Leaves of gelatin are far superior to the powdered product.

This is a perfect dessert to be served with sticks of fresh pineapple which have been marinated in plum brandy.

Gerard's Relais de Lyon

Dinner for Four

Scallops-Jean Banchet

Veal Ciboulette

Escarole Salad

Fresh Kiwi and Strawberries with
Crème de Menthe Sauce

Wine:

With Scallops—Perrier-Jouët Fleur de Champagne, 1973

With Veal—Meursault Les Vireuils, Bernard Morey

With Dessert—Château Caillou Barsac Sauternes, 1970

Gerard Parrat, Owner and Head Chef

Although located outside of Seattle near Bothell, Gerard's must be included among the "city's" finest restaurants. This *relais* (a stop while traveling before going to another city) is just that, and owner Gerard Parrat had such a spot in mind when he opened his restaurant nine years ago—away from the city and in a quiet setting. "I wanted people to come here for dining. Nothing else. Not before or after the theatre."

Gerard and his wife Sharon have created a truly lovely ambiance reminiscent of old country inns, from what was originally an old brick house. The provincial elegance flows from room to room with variations in rich fabrics and colors. Gerard is from Lyon, France, and is dedicated to the culinary heritage of master chef Paul Bocuse, with whom he studied. The entire restaurant, including the service, reveals his dedication to classic French cuisine, presented with care and knowledge. His constant surveillance over the food creates memorable dinners of rich sauces and superlative desserts. He believes in cooking everything from scratch and using proper ingredients. "I believe in freshness and quality in everything."

For a special occasion or a splendid evening away from downtown Seattle, Gerard's complements first-class dining with a comprehensive wine list. Any of the rooms can be used for private parties, and in the summertime, dining on the patio surrounded by lush greenery adds more beauty to an already charming evening.

The inherent refinement in all aspects of this classically French restaurant is a reflection of the owner's devotion. "My work is more important than money. A good chef requires training, long hours, sacrifice and low pay. This is not a job. It is something you have to really want to do or forget it." Gerard has also taught many cooking seminars, and his following of those eager to learn or dine has spread far beyond "out-of-town-Seattle."

17121 Bothell Way Northeast

SCALLOPS-JEAN BANCHET

2 cups cabbage, finely sliced
Butter
Salt and pepper
1 cup heavy cream
2 tablespoons fish glace

1 pound fresh scallops, or
4 large scallops
per person
Cooking oil

1. Sauté cabbage in butter until cooked through but still nice and crisp. Season with salt and pepper. Add the cream and the fish glace. Cook until it is reduced about one-third.
2. Sauté the scallops in very hot oil, a few at a time, allowing about 3 minutes, never more than 5.
3. Place scallops on a plate and top with cabbage mixture.

Always dry scallops thoroughly before they are to be sautéed.

Fish glace may be purchased frozen in some gourmet stores.

I am not in the seasoning business. My base seasonings are salt, pepper, thyme and bay leaf—that is almost all I use. I believe in bones and things rather than seasoning. The taste is always better and I can prove it.

VEAL CIBOULETTE

2 pounds veal bones
1 carrot, coarsely chopped
1 onion, quartered
1 stalk celery, coarsely
 chopped
Salt and pepper
4 Provimi veal chops,
 1" thick

4 tablespoons butter
1 tablespoon oil
1 tablespoon chopped
 shallots
⅓ cup white wine
½ cup whipping cream

1. Prepare veal stock by combining veal bones, carrot, onion and celery

with 3 to 4 quarts of water and simmering for 4 hours or more. Strain and reduce to ½ cup, forming a glace.

2. Salt and pepper the veal chops.

3. Combine 2 tablespoons butter with the oil in a pan and sauté the chops on both sides, approximately 7 to 9 minutes total. Be sure they are not well done and are soft to the touch. Place in a 350° oven for about 3 minutes to cook a bit more. Take meat from the pan and keep warm. Skim off the grease.

4. Add the chopped shallots to the pan in which the chops have been cooked. Sauté and then add white wine. Allow to boil for a few minutes. Add the cream and boil until reduced by one-third. Add the glace and heat, but do not boil again. Turn off heat. Add the remaining 2 tablespoons of butter in small pieces. Shake the pan until the butter is melted, or whip in with a whisk.

5. Place veal on serving plates and top with sauce.

Be sure to turn the heat off before adding the butter pieces. If you don't, the butter will clarify and raise above the sauce. Unsalted butter is best.

I am against thickening sauces with flour, and especially cornstarch. Most of our sauces are done like this one (monte au beurre).

ESCAROLE SALAD

	Escarole greens	½	tablespoon Dijon mustard
6	tablespoons walnut oil		Salt
2	tablespoons red wine vinegar		Pepper

1. Wash and dry greens. Mix remaining ingredients for dressing and toss with escarole in salad bowl.

I only use huile de noix walnut oil from France. It is the very best.

GERARD'S

FRESH KIWI AND STRAWBERRIES
WITH CRÈME DE MENTHE SAUCE

2 kiwi
1 cup strawberries
½ cup sugar
1 cup water

½ cup whipping cream
2 shots crème de menthe
   liqueur

1. Peel the kiwi and slice. Wash strawberries and remove the stems. Slice in halves.
2. Boil the sugar and water to form a syrup and let cool. Add the cream and then the liqueur.
3. Divide the fruit among four dishes and top with sauce.

Substitute peaches or fresh pineapple if kiwis are not available.

Dinner for Four

Fried Brie Cheese

Gazpacho Salad

Pork with Fennel and Lemon

Sautéed Asparagus

Espresso Ice Cream

Wine:

With Brie and Salad—Château Montelena Chardonnay, 1978

With Entrée—Lytton Springs Zinfandel, 1977

With Dessert—Dow's Finest Rare Tawny Port

Karl Beckley, Owner & Chef

"When I started the Grill, I just wanted to serve straightforward food. I look at what's fresh and available." The Greenlake Grill, as described by its owner, is "a new American restaurant emphasizing fresh Northwest ingredients, an exceptionally good wine list and good prices."

The former mom-and-pop-style cafe has been transformed into a dramatic and fresh open space—a perfect prop for this special dining experience. The interior reflects a no-nonsense approach toward all aspects of the business. It is simply understated with black and white checked floors, dark green booths, white tablecloths, grey industrial lamps hung from high ceilings and lots of windows; this in "stark" contrast to the friendliness of the employees and the general din of the customers immersed in fine food, wine and good conversation. "It's progressive, clean, honest and refreshing—not like any other place in town."

The unique subtlety of the Grill stems largely from chef Karl Beckley's demand for quality and his dedication to his own personal style of cooking, one which reflects food under-cooked and flavorful, without the need for heavy sauces and starches. "One of the things that is most appealing to me about this restaurant is what we left out of it. We didn't feel pressured to put things where they weren't necessary."

Well known for stylish and spontaneous presentations of fresh fish, unique shellfish, locally raised game, and pasta dishes, the Grill always offers decadent desserts, and sports a Class H liquor license. In summertime diners may enjoy outside dining. The Greenlake Grill changes its menu quarterly and offers, at the outset of each session, a five-course dinner to introduce the new menu. This allows a chance to highlight some of the new offerings on the menu, themselves a reflection of the changing seasonal abundance of Northwest produce.

"The Grill is just a nice place to come and spend some time. The menu continually changes to accommodate what is fresh and what we know people in Seattle have asked for in the past. We are a *restaurant*, and there is no reason to come here except to enjoy a leisurely meal."

Northeast 72nd and East Green Lake Way

FRIED BRIE CHEESE

1½ pounds 60% Brie cheese
3 tablespoons flour
2 eggs, beaten

½ cup fresh bread crumbs
Peanut oil for frying
TARTAR SAUCE

1. Cut Brie into 1½-inch cubes.
2. Roll in flour to coat; shake off excess flour.
3. Dip in egg.
4. Roll in bread crumbs to coat.
5. Heat 2 inches of peanut oil to 350°. Fry cheese for 2 minutes or until golden brown and melted inside. Serve with TARTAR SAUCE.

TARTAR SAUCE

3 egg yolks
2 teaspoons Pommery
     mustard
3 tablespoons lemon juice
1 tablespoon champagne
     vinegar

2 tablespoons capers
10 cornichons
     Salt and pepper
1 cup peanut oil

1. Place all ingredients except oil in food processor.
2. Turn on and add oil in a slow stream. If you don't have a food processor, chop the capers and corichons and use an electric mixer or wire whip.

The pursuit of detail is the religion of success.

This place is not for people who need security; it's adverturesome and you've got to be able to trust the people who work here because so many intriguing menu items need explaining.

GAZPACHO SALAD

1 green pepper, cut in strips
1 cucumber, cut in half and
then in strips
2 tomatoes, cut in wedges

1 small red onion, cut in
strips
DRESSING

Place all ingredients in a bowl and toss with DRESSING.

DRESSING

6 cloves garlic, chopped
1½ tablespoons chopped
shallots
3 pinches cumin

Large pinch chopped
parsley
Salt and pepper
¼ cup red wine vinegar
½ cup olive oil

1. Place all dry ingredients in bowl.
2. Add vinegar.
3. Slowly add oil in a stream while whipping with a wire whisk.

Being a great chef does not come from being at it a long time or from classical training. What makes a good or great chef is probably the opportunities he gets.

The thing that makes this restaurant have good food is that we're not concerned with operating in an established mode. We didn't label ourselves.

I don't believe our location makes us a great deal more successful than we are. It's important for exposure, but not important if you don't have the product.

PORK WITH FENNEL AND LEMON

1½ pounds pork tenderloin
   Salt and pepper
½ teaspoon ground fennel
   seed
   Olive oil

1 stalk fresh fennel, chopped
3 ounces brandy
3 lemons
2 cups cream

1. Have your butcher "de-nude" the pork. Cut into 1-inch thick slices and pound them to ½-inch thickness.
2. Season with salt, pepper and ground fennel seed.
3. Fry in a small amount of olive oil on high heat for 2 minutes. Turn and cook another 2 minutes. Remove to a platter and keep warm.
4. Degrease the pan, then add the fresh fennel and brandy. Reduce.
5. Zest the lemons and reserve. Cut lemons in half and squeeze the juice into the pan. Add the cream. Reduce to the consistency of heavy cream.
6. Test for seasoning, add the lemon zest and serve over the pork.

In educating our staff, we believe our waiters are just a small part of the experience. They are not actors; they don't play the part of entertaining the table. They are there to provide service. They are not to be at the table when they're not needed. It's a sensitivity not to intrude on a conversation.

SAUTÉED ASPARAGUS

1¼ pounds fresh asparagus
4 tablespoons butter

Salt and pepper

1. Trim and wash asparagus.
2. Sauté in butter over medium heat for 7 minutes. Season with salt and pepper.

The hardest part of preparing a meal at home is getting everything together at one time, organizing it so I can still move in the kitchen.

Poor management is the reason 99.9% of businesses go under. We are here at all times; we are management intensive. We pay a lot of attention and put a lot of energy into not being one of those statistics.

ESPRESSO ICE CREAM

Makes 1 gallon

2½ cups sugar
¼ teaspoon salt
2 tablespoons flour
2½ cups hot espresso coffee
2½ cups half and half

1 vanilla bean, split
  lengthwise
6 egg yolks
5 cups heavy cream

1. With a wire whisk, mix together sugar, salt, flour, hot espresso, half and half and vanilla bean until well combined.
2. Add egg yolks and cream, mixing well.
3. Freeze in ice cream freezer according to manufacturer's instructions.
4. Before serving, remove vanilla bean.

The hardest parts of being owners are satisfying employees and managing one's time well enough to not burn one's self out on the restaurant business and the everyday details. The pursuit of details is everything. After that, the everyday things take care of themselves.

Henry's off Broadway

Dinner for Four

Oysters Rockefeller

Celery Almond Soup

Jackson Square Salad

Marchand de Vin

Bananas Flambé

Wine:

With Oysters—Piesporter Goldtröpfchen

With Chicken—a Beaujolais-Villages

With Bananas—Schramsberg Cremant Champagne

Bill Schwartz and John Henry Schwartz, Owners

Jon Sheard, General Manager

HENRY'S OFF BROADWAY

When Henry's off Broadway opened in June, 1977, after two years of planning and over one million dollars invested, it was an instant success. The restaurant is named after John Henry Schwartz, the general manager of all ten restaurants that he and his brother Bill own, but the ideas and plans behind Henry's were a group effort.

The whole thing started with the first Butcher restaurant, which opened in Bellevue's Benaroya Business Park in October, 1970. What had started out as a "convenience" to the businessmen of the area turned out to be a million dollar business within the first year. This initial success spawned the Sandwich Shops in Seattle, Tukwila, and Bellevue, a second Butcher restaurant in the Design Center-Northwest, Daniel's Broiler, and Benjamin's in Bellevue, Seattle and Portland.

Henry's off Broadway, a Travel/Holiday magazine award winner, is the most unusual of the ten restaurants. The contemporary casualness of all the others has been set aside, and a comfortable, elegant Continental feeling of the 1930's has been established. Most of the furnishings and fabrics have been imported: the drapes from France, the sumptuous green velvet on the booths from Holland, the frames for the cane chairs from France, the crystal on the chandeliers and the marble on the tables from Italy, and the wool carpet from England. The Oyster Bar Lounge features an exquisite etched glass grand piano "set" like a diamond in a rose-marble piano bar.

"We wanted Henry's to be THE restaurant," says John Schwartz. "The city needed another elegant restaurant, and we set out to fill that need by providing a total dining experience for the customer. From the time that the valet meets the car, to the reception received at the front desk, to the waiter at the table, we strive for impeccable service. We use the highest quality food products, cut our own veal, and buy the best coffee and liquors. Henry's is a success, but we're always changing to make it better."

1705 East Olive Way

OYSTERS ROCKEFELLER

1 *pound chopped spinach*	2 *teaspoons garlic powder*
1 *tablespoon butter*	2 *teaspoons Season-All*
1 *tablespoon flour*	1 *pound fresh oysters*
½ *cup half and half*	*Rock salt*
2 to 3 *strips bacon, finely chopped*	1½ *cups Hollandaise sauce*
1½ *tablespoons shallots, peeled and diced*	*Lemon wedges*
	Parsley sprigs
2 *ounces Swiss cheese, grated*	

1. Cook spinach and drain well. Set aside.

2. Melt butter in small saucepan and stir in flour. Add half-and-half, stirring until smooth. Continue cooking, stirring constantly, until mixture thickens and bubbles. Set aside.

3. Sauté bacon on medium heat approximately 2 minutes. Add shallots and sauté an additional 2 minutes. Add drained spinach and white sauce. When thoroughly mixed, add Swiss cheese and stir until cheese is completely melted. Season with garlic powder and Season-All. Set aside.

4. Open oysters and cut muscles holding them to their shells. Wash oysters and return to cleaned half shells. Place approximately 1 to 1½ ounces spinach mixture on each oyster and spread evenly.

5. In a shallow cookie pan, spread out a thin layer of rock salt. Place prepared oysters on rock salt and place in 500° oven for approximately 10 to 12 minutes. Remove from oven and place six oysters on each of four preheated plates. Ladle approximately 1 tablespoon Hollandaise sauce over each oyster and serve garnished with lemon wedges and parsley sprigs.

One of Henry's most popular features is the 50 foot, marble-topped oyster bar, where customers can order seafood and other specialties and watch as they are prepared at the open grill in front of them.

We spent a lot of time researching the oyster bar. Ours isn't like any other; it has its own personality.

CELERY ALMOND SOUP

5 stalks celery, minced
¼ cup butter
2 tablespoons slivered
   almonds

¼ cup flour
6 cups chicken stock
1½ pints whipping cream

1. Melt butter in saucepan and add celery. Sauté on medium heat until tender, approximately 5 minutes. Add almonds and slowly sift flour in, stirring constantly until thoroughly mixed.
2. Stir in chicken stock and simmer on medium heat 20 minutes. Remove from heat and let cool for 5 minutes.
3. Place mixture in blender or food processor and purée until smooth. Place in refrigerator and chill for 2 hours.
4. When ready to serve, add 1 pint whipping cream to chilled soup. Whip remaining ½ pint whipping cream until stiff. Divide soup among chilled soup cups and garnish with a dollop of whipped cream.

We have an excellent chef who pays personal attention to the highest quality products.

JACKSON SQUARE SALAD

1 large head romaine
1 avocado
¼ pound peeled Alaskan
   baby shrimp
¼ pound Dungeness crab
   meat
2 ounces Roquefort cheese,
   crumbled

DRESSING
2 tomatoes, quartered
12 olives
2 hard-cooked eggs,
   shredded

1. Wash and dry romaine, then chill. Cut into 1-inch pieces and place in salad bowl. Peel avocado, remove pit and cut into ½-inch dice.

Add to romaine, along with shrimp, crab meat and Roquefort cheese.

2. Add Dressing and toss gently until all ingredients are thoroughly coated. Divide among four chilled salad plates and garnish with tomato wedges, olives and shredded eggs.

DRESSING

1 egg
½ teaspoon anchovy paste
1 clove garlic, crushed and minced
1 tablespoon Grey Poupon mustard
1 cup olive oil

¼ cup red wine vinegar
½ teaspoon Worcestershire sauce
Juice of ¼ lemon
Salt
Freshly ground pepper

1. Mix together egg, anchovy paste, garlic and mustard. Slowly beat in olive oil. You should have a mixture with a mayonnaise-like consistency.

2. Add vinegar and Worcestershire sauce and mix thoroughly. Stir in lemon juice; add salt and pepper to taste.

MARCHAND DE VIN

5 tablespoons unsalted butter
1 shallot, minced
½ pound mushrooms, quartered
½ cup Burgundy wine

¼ teaspoon whole thyme
1 cup demi-glace (or brown sauce)
2 tablespoons olive oil
4 chicken breasts
Flour

1. Sauté minced shallot in 1 tablespoon butter until transparent. Add mushrooms and sauté until soft. Add wine and whole thyme. Bring

to a boil, then simmer until reduced by half, approximately 5 minutes. Gently stir in demi-glace thoroughly and simmer an additional 10 minutes.

2. While sauce is simmering, heat olive oil in another pan on medium heat. Lightly flour chicken breasts and sauté in oil until golden brown on both sides.

3. Remove sauce from heat and stir in 4 tablespoons unsalted butter until sauce is smooth and velvety.

4. Place chicken breasts in a deep-dish baking pan and cover with sauce. Cover pan and place in a 350° oven for 20 minutes.

5. Remove from oven and place chicken on heated platter. Add an additional tablespoon of wine to sauce and stir until smooth. Pour sauce over chicken and serve.

We suggest you serve this dish with sautéed carrots and Parisienne potatoes.

BANANAS FLAMBÉ

4 tablespoons butter	2 teaspoons ground cinnamon
½ cup brown sugar	
1 ounce orange juice	4 scoops vanilla ice cream
4 ripe bananas	Shredded coconut, almonds or pecans (optional)
1¼ ounces banana liqueur	
1 ounce orange Curacao	
1½ ounces 151° Lemon Hart rum	

1. Heat a shallow pan until hot. Add butter, brown sugar and orange juice. Stir with a large spoon until completely mixed and smooth.

2. Peel bananas and cut in half lengthwise. Add bananas to sauce and add banana liqueur and orange Curacao. Continue stirring sauce while ladling over bananas. Turn bananas twice, then add 151° rum. Be extremely careful when adding rum; when flame begins, pull container away immediately. As the dish is flaming, sprinkle cinna-

mon over the bananas. Carefully continue to ladle flaming sauce over the bananas. Using the large spoon, cut the bananas in half. When doing this, check for the tenderness of the bananas. If the spoon goes through easily, you want to take the bananas out immediately. If they are stll rather firm, cook another 30 seconds or so.

3. Put 1 scoop vanilla ice cream in the middle of each chilled plate. Arrange bananas around the ice cream. The sauce should be rather bubbly and caramelized. If not, add ½ ounce more banana liqueur and stir. Raise the heat if necessary. When the sauce is caramelized, ladle it over the ice cream. Top with shredded coconut, almonds or pecans if desired.

The employees are the restaurant. We hire the best people, give them a proper orientation, and teach them how to give good service to our customers.

McCORMICK'S
FISH HOUSE & BAR

Dinner for Four

Wescott Bay International Petite Oysters on the Half-Shell

Tossed Salad with Creamy Vinaigrette Dressing

King Salmon with Brandy and Peach Sauce

Carrots and Sugar Snap Peas Sauté

Raspberry Sherbet

Wine:

With Oysters—Korbel Brut champagne

With Salad—Concannon Sauvignon Blanc

With Salmon—Chablis Premier Cru, Fourchaume, J. Vercherre

After Dinner—Graham's Vintage Port, 1970

Bill McCormick, Owner

Paul Gould, Chef

Steve Gabica, General Manager

S itting in McCormick's very quickly transports one back in time and place: the feeling and atmosphere are that of the standard, old-time Boston or New York fish house. Church pews, reminiscent of the late 1800s, with practical and charming coat trees attached, face each other to create most of the seating in the restaurant in private, booth-like units.

Milk-glass school lamps with long brass stems hang from the ceiling, and milk-glass tulip lamps light the tables. Everywhere are framed old photographs, sheet music, and posters. The metal tiles forming the ceiling, the stained glass, and the use of mahogany, oak, and maple in abundance help to complete the feeling of warmth and comfort. "It's an Irish place," states Steve Gabica, the manager, and indeed it is.

McCormick's, bearing the name of owner Bill McCormick, is located in a building constructed in 1912. The philosophy for McCormick's restaurant is stated on the menu: "We take pride in presenting only the highest quality food, prepared totally on the premises." Steve Gabica explains that everything possible is prepared with fresh ingredients. "We have a very small freezer, and we don't work out of cans or boxes." McCormick's has what Steve calls a "living menu." "Our entire menu is reprinted each day, thus reflecting daily and seasonal changes in the availability of fresh foods. We try to keep our menu interesting. We also feel the responsibility to educate, to make available new seafoods for people to try." No gimmicks in food or service are allowed. Everything is kept simple on purpose. "McCormick's is probably the same place it's been for ten years. It's a very traditional restaurant, and it is this consistency which keeps people coming back year after year."

In October, 1984, Bill and partner Doug Schmick opened a second restaurant, McCormick and Schmick's. While quite different in format, price structure and menu variety, McCormick & Schmick's continues the high emphasis on fresh seafood which has placed McCormick's among the city's favorite dining establishments.

The style of McCormick's is not to impress or overwhelm its guests. "We're not trying to dazzle anyone with our saucework or fancy-name dishes," explains Steve. "You don't come here for a romantic, candlelight dinner." McCormick's is a busy, noisy restaurant, and one of the finest places in a seafood town for seafood.

722 4th Avenue
1103 1st Avenue

WESCOTT BAY INTERNATIONAL PETIT OYSTERS ON THE HALF-SHELL

16 fresh Wescott Bay
   oysters
1 lemon, cut in wedges

Parsley sprigs
Tabasco sauce

1. Shuck the oysters just prior to serving, taking care not to damage the delicate meat inside. Be sure to clear the abductor muscle from the bottom of the shell so that the oyster can be easily removed.
2. Serve the oysters on the half-shell, set into shaved ice, four to a plate. Garnish with lemon wedges and parsley sprigs and serve Tabasco sauce on the side.

Cocktail sauce may be used, but it would be a shame to mask the flavor of these oysters.

Wescott Bay oysters are grown off San Juan Island. The International Petite is a hybrid cross between the Pacific and the Japanese Kumomoto. These oysters are grown in nets off the floor of the bay and develop a higher meat-to-shell ratio than dredged or raked oysters.

TOSSED SALAD

⅓ head iceberg lettuce
⅓ head romaine lettuce
⅓ head Bibb lettuce
   CREAMY VINAIGRETTE
   DRESSING

CROUTONS
1 tomato, sliced
½ cucumber, sliced
½ cup black olives

1. Wash and dry the lettuces. Tear the leaves into bite-size pieces.
2. Place the lettuce in a salad bowl and toss gently with the Creamy Vinaigrette Dressing.
3. Portion the salad onto four salad plates. Garnish with Croutons, tomato slices, cucumber slices, and a few black olives.

CREAMY VINAIGRETTE DRESSING

1 tablespoon chopped fresh
   basil
½ tablespoon chopped fresh
   tarragon
   Juice of ½ lemon

2 cloves garlic, pressed
1 tablespoon Dijon mustard
¼ cup red wine vinegar
1 egg
1 cup olive oil

1. In a small bowl, beat the fresh herbs, lemon juice, garlic, and mustard with the vinegar and set aside.
2. In a medium bowl, whip the egg vigorously for 30 seconds; begin gradually adding the oil and then the vinegar mixture until the dressing achieves the consistency of thin mayonnaise.

Fresh herbs will give more flavor if beaten with the vinegar rather than the oil or egg.

CROUTONS

¼ loaf sourdough bread

4 tablespoons butter

Cube the bread and fry until golden in the butter. Drain.

KING SALMON WITH BRANDY AND PEACH SAUCE

¼ pound butter
2 pounds king salmon
   belly meat, trimmed
   and cut into 1" slices
4 fresh peaches, sliced
   in half-moon slices
1 cup julienne-cut leeks,
   1½" long

1 tablespoon chopped
   fresh parsley
   Juice of ½ lemon
1½ ounces brandy
¾ cup heavy cream
4 to 6 cups steamed white rice

1. In a large skillet, melt 4 tablespoons butter over medium heat. When the butter has melted and begins to foam, add the salmon. Sauté for about 30 seconds , then add the peaches, leeks, parsley, and lemon juice. Increase the heat and sauté for 45 to 60 seconds.
2. Flame with brandy. After the flame dies, add the cream. Reduce by one-half.
3. Remove from heat and gently stir in the remaining butter to incorporate. Serve at once over steamed white rice.

King salmon is a name given to large chinook salmon. The belly meat is used for this dish due to its high fat content.

CARROTS AND SUGAR SNAP PEAS SAUTÉ

4 *medium-size carrots*	*White pepper to taste*
1 *pound sugar snap peas*	*Salt to taste*
¼ *cup olive oil*	1 *clove garlic, very*
¼ *cup vermouth*	*finely chopped*

1. Cut the carrots into julienne pieces, 1½ inches long and as thin as possible. Steam only until they lose their snap and reach their peak of color, about 1½ to 2 minutes.
2. Wash the peas. Heat the olive oil in a sauté pan until hot. Add the carrots and peas; sauté for 1 to 2 minutes, or just until the peas have reached their peak in color. Deglaze the pan with the vermouth and remove from heat.
3. Season the vegetables with pepper, salt, and garlic.

I like this vegetable combination because it is delicious and adds real color to the plate.

RASPBERRY SHERBET

2 pints fresh raspberries,
   or 1 (10-ounce) package
   frozen
¾ cup sugar

½ cup corn syrup
¼ cup fresh lemon juice
2 egg whites
Mint leaves

1. Reserve several whole raspberries as garnish. Purée the remainder in a food processor or blender.
2. Dissolve the sugar in 1 cup warm water. Stir in the corn syrup, lemon juice, and raspberry purée.
3. Place this mixture in the freezer and freeze until it sets firm around the edges.
4. In a separate bowl, beat the egg whites until stiff.
5. Turn the partially frozen raspberry mixture in its bowl, then fold in the egg whites.
6. Spoon into individual sorbet glasses and return to the freezer.
7. At serving time, garnish with the reserved raspberries and fresh mint leaves.

MIRABEAU

Dinner for Six

Cream Cheese Jalapeño

Prawns with Pernod

Hears of Romaine with Avocado Dressing

Country Duck with Turnips

Amaretto Parfait

Wine:

With Prawns and Salad—Beaulieu Vineyards Chablis

With Duck—Château Talbot

With Dessert—Niersteiner

Gilbert Barthe, Owner

Jacki Bonnet, Chef

THE MIRABEAU

From high atop a skyscraper, the view of Puget Sound, the Olympic Mountains, and the expanse of buildings and streets that create downtown Seattle is magnificent. Gilbert Barthe, the convivial owner and manager of the Mirabeau, has proudly claimed occupancy of the 46th floor of the Seattle First National Bank Building since it opened 16 years ago. "We're the tallest restaurant in Seattle," he asserts, "even higher than the Space Needle."

Gilbert Barthe learned to cook in the country kitchen of his grandmother, who worked for a baron in the Toulouse area of southwestern France. He moved to Canada in 1953 and in later years to California, where he worked as fry cook, bus boy, waiter, captain and manager in various restaurants. He feels, knowing the restaurant business as he does, that his Mirabeau is a success because he is there 14 hours a day, sometimes six days a week. "I arrive at the restaurant each day, go immediately into the kitchen, and begin tasting. This is how the quality is maintained."

The Mirabeau started out as a French restaurant, but Gilbert Barthe's love of the Pacific Northwest and its game birds and seafoods is reflected in the menu of today. If a customer brings him a freshly caught duck or quail, Barthe will prepare it for him in the Mirabeau kitchen. He is uncommonly eager to please. He caters to the special diets of special patrons and says, "I believe a satisfied customer is the only reason for our existence. Should anything not be to your liking, please tell us in time to correct our error."

1001 4th Avenue, 46th Floor

CREAM CHEESE JALAPENO

8 ounces cream cheese
6 ounces hot jalapeño jelly

Parsley or grapes
Crackers

Cover cream cheese with jalapeño jelly and garnish with parsley sprigs or grapes. Serve with plain crackers.

This will make a very easy but quite interesting cocktail hors d'oeuvre.

When friends dine at my house, I want to enjoy the company. It's hard to have six perfect, complicated courses. I usually concentrate on one difficult course and keep the rest of the meal quite simple so that I can be with my guests.

PRAWNS WITH PERNOD

12 large prawns, shelled and
    deveined
   Flour
 2 tablespoons butter

2 ounces Pernod
1 cup whipping cream
1½ teaspoons chopped parsley
   Salt and pepper

1. Split prawns lengthwise and flour lightly. Sauté in butter for 3 to 4 minutes.
2. Add Pernod to pan and flambé. Add whipping cream, parsley, salt and pepper. Bring to a quick boil while stirring. Serve at once.

If sauce is too thin, add ½ teaspoon cornstarch diluted in water. Bring to a boil once again.

HEARTS OF ROMAINE WITH AVOCADO DRESSING

2 *heads romaine*
  AVOCADO DRESSING

1 to 2 *hard-cooked eggs,*
  chopped

1. Trim outer leaves from romaine. Cut each romaine heart in half.
2. Place hearts on individual chilled salad plates and top with Avocado Dressing. Sprinkle chopped eggs over top.

AVOCADO DRESSING

1 *cup oil*
⅓ *cup red wine vinegar*
½ *clove garlic*

½ *avocado*
1 *raw egg*
  Salt and pepper to taste

Blend on high speed for 2 minutes.

COUNTRY DUCK WITH TURNIPS

1 *domestic duck, 4 to*
  5 pounds
  Salt and pepper
3 *cloves garlic*
2 *glasses red wine*

½ *cup black olives*
½ *cup green olives*
6 *medium turnips, peeled*
  and cut into
  ¾" wedges

1. Prick skin all over duck to encourage unwanted fat to run out. Sprinkle with salt and pepper. Place 2 cloves garlic inside duck cavity.
2. Set duck on a rack in a large pan so grease will not touch the bird. Cook at 475° for 30 minutes. Remove duck from pan and reserve grease.

3. Place duck into a fireproof pot with a tight fitting lid, adding wine and remaining clove of garlic. Cover and cook slowly in 325° oven for 45 minutes, just allowing it to simmer.

4. Remove duck from roasting pan and carve into four pieces. Add juices to the pan with the wine. With a turkey baster, remove the fat which has collected on top of the wine. Taste the sauce for seasoning. If the duck is still too pink, put it back in the oven until done. If it is done, add olives to the pan just long enough to warm—but not cook—them.

5. Meanwhile, prepare turnips by boiling in salted water approximately 4 minutes, or until tender yet crisp. Drain and dry. Brown lightly in leftover duck grease.

6. Serve duck with turnips.

The duck can be prepared before the guests arrive, cooled, and then warmed up at the last minute. If you are preparing wild duck, you needn't roast the original 30 minutes since they are smaller and have very little fat.

Left-over duck grease can be used instead of butter to prepare vegetables at a later date. This is especially good with baked beans, lentils, split peas and lima beans.

The turnips can be partially boiled in advance and then sautéed just before serving.

AMARETTO PARFAIT

1 scoop vanilla ice cream	1 heaping tablespoon
½ ounce Amaretto	whipped cream
	Slivered almonds

Place scoops of your best vanilla ice cream in individual champagne coupes or tulip glasses. Top with Amaretto, whipped cream and slivered almonds.

If you make ahead of time and keep in the freezer, add liquor just before serving. The flavor will be better.

1904

Dinner for Four

Carpaccio

Spinach and Walnut Salad

Fettuccini Primavera

Salmon with Three-Mustard Sauce

Italian Fruit Tart

Wine:

With Carpaccio—Gattinara, Travilgini, 1979

With Salmon—Chalone Chardonnay, 1983

With Tart—Domaine Chandon Brut

*David Holt, Illsley Nordstrom, Paul Schell,
& Jim Youngren, Owners*

Mickey McEachern, Manager

Steve Debaste, Kitchen Manager

1904

Sleek, uncluttered, functional, and not a fern or a potted palm in sight. "The people are the plants," says David Holt, one of the owners of 1904, a restaurant with a real urban ambiance. "We intentionally created a stark space; we wanted the people, and not the ferns, to be the atmosphere, to give the restaurant personality."

"Seattle has had restaurants downtown," according to Holt, "but not downtown restaurants." Since the day it opened in 1980, 1904 has been trying to fill a void in the Seattle dining scene. "We are pioneering," explains Holt. "Here is a place where people come and things happen. It is a real gathering place, a place to meet and exchange ideas." Lunchtime in particular finds attorneys, architects, politicians, developers, and others, representing many different lifestyles and careers, conducting business, conversing, and enjoying a creatively prepared meal.

Gordon Walker received a National Architecture Award for his work on the interior of the building at 1904 Fourth Avenue, which was originally constructed in 1906 and is listed in the historical register. The design is unique. A massive wine bar creates the center of the restaurant; it is constructed, as is the staircase leading to the upstairs, of glass bricks, with neon behind, and industrial pipe. From this wine bar, 65 wines by the bottle and 32 by the glass are available.

Dinner at 1904 provides a choice of elegant appetizers, including carpaccio, escargot, and pâté, and features fresh pasta—including the house specialty, prepared with smoked salmon, crème fraîche and scotch—in addition to meat, fish, and poultry entrées. "It's actually a pretty straightforward presentation," claims Holt. "We try to avoid fancy names and high prices, and we do not buy anything in a bottle." All of the dressings, stocks, desserts, and "the best bread in town" are made in the restaurant.

1904 has just recently been responsible for the opening of Italia, an Italian market and cafe in Cornerstone's new Waterfront Center. Naturally, Italia, too, carries on the fine tradition and philosophy of 1904. Today, with the ongoing revitalization of the downtown of Seattle, 1904 is in the middle of things, and that seems appropriate for a "downtown" restaurant.

1904 4th Avenue

CARPACCIO

1½ pounds top sirloin roast
1 pint SAUCE

⅔ cup fresh grated
Parmesan cheese

1. Cut the top sirloin roast, with the grain, into logs, 1½ to 2 inches in diameter. Wrap the beef tightly in aluminum foil and freeze. When the meat is frozen, remove and slice into discs as thinly as possible. The more frozen the meat, the easier it is to slice. The meat should be so thin that it is semi-transparent.
2. Arrange the thin discs of meat around the perimeter of a small plate and spread the Sauce in the center of the plate so that it covers the exposed part of the plate.
3. Top sparingly with freshly grated Parmesan cheese and serve.

SAUCE

2 egg yolks
1 cup olive oil
6 cloves garlic, minced
2 tablespoons Worcestershire
   sauce

¼ cup red wine vinegar
1 teaspoon salt
¼ cup Dijon mustard

1. Proceed as for mayonnaise: whisk the egg yolks until well blended (or blend in a blender), then slowly drizzle in the olive oil.
2. Add the remaining ingredients and blend to amalgamate.

1904

SPINACH AND WALNUT SALAD

2 large bunches fresh spinach
2 cups iceberg lettuce,
   cut in julienne

1¼ cups toasted walnuts,
   skins removed

DRESSING

1. Thoroughly wash and dry the spinach. (If water is left on the spinach, the dressing won't cling to the leaves and also will become diluted.)
2. Break the spinach into bite-size pieces and place in a salad bowl.
3. Add the julienned lettuce and 1 cup toasted walnuts.
4. Toss the greens and walnuts with the Dressing. Garnish with the reserved toasted walnuts and serve.

DRESSING

2 teaspoons Dijon mustard
2 tablespoons white wine
   vinegar
¼ cup walnut oil

2 tablespoons vegetable oil
Coarse black pepper
   to taste
Coarse salt to taste

Blend all ingredients together thoroughly.

All of our salads, whether they be spinach, Bibb lettuce, or romaine, are hand torn and towel dried. The more moisture left on the greens, the less impact the dressing will have. People generally don't spend enough time on this step.

FETTUCCINI PRIMAVERA

6 tablespoons olive oil
2 tablespoons butter
½ medium-size onion,
  thinly sliced
1 sweet red pepper,
  thinly sliced
1 bunch asparagus, cut
  in 2" lengths and
  blanched

½ head broccoli, cut
  into florets and blanched
1 cup fresh peas
½ pound fresh fettuccini
⅓ cup dry vermouth
  Freshly ground black
  pepper to taste
  Freshly grated Parmesan
  cheese

1. Fill a large pot with water, add ¼ cup olive oil, and bring to a rapid boil.
2. Meanwhile, heat the butter and the remaining 2 tablespoons olive oil in a large sauté pan. Add the onion and sweet red pepper. Lightly sauté.
3. Add the remaining vegetables. Sauté over high heat, tossing continuously.
4. When the vegetables are almost tender, place the pasta in the boiling water. Boil gently for 2 to 3 minutes, or until al dente—soft but with a hint of firmness when bitten.
5. At this point, the vegetables should be crisp-tender. Add the vermouth and continue cooking for 1 to 2 minutes more.
6. Drain the pasta as the vegetables complete their cooking.
7. Toss the vegetables with the fettuccini, adding black pepper to taste. Garnish with grated Parmesan cheese and serve immediately.

The amount of time needed to cook fresh pasta varies greatly, depending on the age, the moisture content, and the quality of the pasta.

SALMON WITH THREE-MUSTARD SAUCE

1 cup *FISH FUMET*
   (see page 127) or stock
½ cup *dry white wine*
4 *(6- to 8-ounce) fresh*
   salmon filets
1½ cups *heavy cream*
1 heaping tablespoon
   Dijon mustard

1 heaping tablespoon
   Pommery mustard
1 heaping tablespoon
   tarragon mustard
1 tablespoon chopped
   fresh tarragon
1 tablespoon *butter, cold*

1. Preheat the oven to 200°.
2. In a large frying pan, heat the Fish Fumet and white wine until simmering. Add the salmon filets, skin side up. Simmer the salmon for 3 to 5 minutes, then turn over.
3. Discard ½ cup of the Fumet, and add the cream. Bring the mixture to a slow boil. Boil gently for 3 to 4 minutes, or until the fish is firm.
4. Remove the salmon and place in a shallow boat dish. Place the fish in the preheated oven until ready to serve.
5. Continue reducing the cream sauce until it thickens enough to cling to the salmon when served. Add the mustards and the tarragon. Blend together over low heat until incorporated.
6. Add the cold butter to finish the sauce. Remove the pan from the heat and swirl the sauce until the butter has melted. Pour over the salmon and serve.

ITALIAN FRUIT TART

1½ cups *ricotta cheese*
5 tablespoons *sugar*
1 tablespoon *orange liqueur*
   Zest of 1 orange
1 tablespoon grated
   semi-sweet chocolate

SWEET PÂTE BRISÉE
2 pints *fresh berries*
1 cup *red currant jelly*

1. Using a food processor, blend together the ricotta cheese, sugar, orange liqueur, orange zest, and grated chocolate.
2. Smooth the filling into the cooled tart shell.
3. Top with the fresh berries.
4. Heat the currant jelly with 1 tablespoon water to make a glaze. Drizzle the glaze over the berries.

SWEET PÂTE BRISÉE

1¼ cups flour	6 tablespoons cold butter, cut into small cubes
¼ teaspoon salt	
2 teaspoons sugar	1 tablespoon cold margarine

1. Preheat oven to 400°.
2. Combine the flour and the salt in the large bowl of an electric mixer. Add the sugar. With the mixer running, add the cold butter and margarine and then 3 to 4 tablespoons ice water, a tablespoon at a time, until the dough begins to cohere.
3. Chill the dough before rolling to fill an 11-inch tart pan.
4. Bake in preheated oven for 10 to 15 minutes.

You can take advantage of whatever fruit is in season, as we do at 1904. Be adventuresome by using fresh blackberries, strawberries, raspberries, blueberries, or huckleberries; even apples, pears, or peaches would be wonderful in this dessert.

Rosellini's
OTHER PLACE

Dinner for Six

Red King Salmon Baked in a Paper Case with Sorrel

Pear and Rosehip Ice

Grilled Filet Steak with Chive Butter

Turnip Purée

Salad of Seasonal Greens

Blueberry Tart

Wine:

With Salmon—Meursault Les Casses-Têtes, Thévènin, 1976

With Steak—Echézeaux Leroy, 1967

With Tarte—Château Rieussec Sauternes, 1976

Robert Rosellini, Owner

THE OTHER PLACE

A classic in its own right, Rosellini's Other Place is a reflection of Robert Rosellini's individuality, exemplifying his personal philosophy as well as his comprehensive and diversified restaurant background. Besides having studied in Europe in several restaurants, and at several butcher shops, trout and vegetable farms, Robert's genuine love of food, wine and people is what makes the actual mechanics of restaurant business appear effortless for him. "Quality is the window I look through to do everything."

Inconspicuously located in the middle of downtown Seattle, The Other Place exudes an atmosphere of elegance—from white linen, rich green booths, leather captain's chairs and high ceilings, to classical music and the small, intimate bar. "I like the elegance, quietness, professionalism and formality of French service. The environment here *does* define what it is all about; and although rigid, it gives people the opportunity to play this game and have fun doing it."

The serious and thorough wine list accompanies a continually changing seasonal menu. The strict regional cuisine is inspired by classical French techniques but is mainly dedicated to the integrity of the ingredients used, the quality of the base product. The team of chefs befriends local farmers to insure the best organically grown produce. "We deal with farming 'artists' who grow produce for flavor and not for mass production. They employ care, love, and knowledge."

Rosellini's thoughts on the making of a great restaurant pay tribute to the individual functioning in an environment which promotes creativity and brilliance. "I have a need to make a contribution to the quality of life around me, and it has to express itself through a medium; the restaurant is a wonderful opportunity to demonstrate what quality is all about and to express humanity to the community."

Gourmets cannot help but praise the noble aspirations for elegant atmosphere and indigenous fare. Perhaps they have much to do with his success. Victor Rosellini professed to his son: "I have a great restaurant because my customers are great."

319 Union Street

RED KING SALMON BAKED IN A PAPER CASE WITH SORREL

½ cup unsalted butter, melted

6 pieces cooking parchment paper

6 4-ounce salmon filets

¾ cup fresh sorrel, coarsely cut

2 tablespoons solid unsalted butter

2 lemons

Salt

Fresh ground white pepper

1. Brush the work surface with a little melted butter. Place a piece of cooking parchment on surface and brush top with melted butter. Place a salmon filet a little off center of sheet. On top of filet, place about 2 tablespoons chopped sorrel, 1 teaspoon butter, a squeeze of lemon juice, a pinch of salt and a quick grind of white pepper. Fold the paper over the filet, forming a triangle. Fold edges in to seal sides. The butter on both sides of the paper will help to make a seal. Repeat for other filets.

2. Place salmon filets on an oiled baking sheet and bake in a very hot (500°) oven for 6 minutes or until puffed and brown. Serve immediately by splitting open the top.

A wonderful perfume comes forth when you open the packets.

If you have great customers, you will perform at the level that they are willing to be great.

PEAR AND ROSEHIP ICE

3 pears

½ cup rose hips

1 quart organic pear juice

1. Peel and core the pears. Break up the rose hips. Cook the pears and rosehips over medium heat in the pear juice until well cooked. Pears will be soft.

2. By raising the heat, reduce the volume of the liquid by one-third for the flavor to intensify. Pass through the finest mesh sieve, pressing hard to extract all juice and even to obtain some of the pulp for texture.

3. Freeze, stirring occasionally with a wire whisk about every 15 minutes to assure a homogeneous texture. When frozen, serve by shaping the golden crystals into a chilled wine glass.

Roses produce their fruits in autumn. The rose hips will give this a nice gold-red color.

Recipes are instructional but not creative; they are not in the process of learning about food. You don't get there by a recipe. Training is a process and you must utilize the information you have rather than work out of it. The main ingredient is paying attention—the recipe for all recipes.

GRILLED FILET STEAK WITH CHIVE BUTTER

6 *8-ounce filet steaks*
¾ *cup Madeira wine*
3 *tablespoons wine vinegar*
3 *shallots, minced*

4½ *tablespoons chopped chives*
2 *cubes unsalted butter, at room temperature*

1. In a stainless steel pan, boil the Madeira, vinegar, shallots and 1½ tablespoons chives until it is reduced to one-third of its former volume.

2. Blanch remaining 3 tablespoons chives and set aside.

3. Cut butter into small pieces. Take pan off heat and, while still warm, beat in the butter with a wire whisk, piece by piece, to form an emulsion with a creamy consistency. Pass through a fine chinoise (fine wire mesh, as fine as cheesecloth). Add the blanched chives and keep warm.

4. Flatten the steaks slightly. Grill 3 to 4 minutes per side. Serve with chive butter and Turnip Purée.

Make sure the reduction is not too hot or the butter will simply melt and not form the velvety consistency which is desired.

The best way to grill the steak at home is on a heavy iron skillet which has raised ridges on the bottom. Put a small amount of oil on both sides of the steak.

We get the best quality beef—western Washington organically grown beef (with no antibiotics or hormones injected), which has been dry aged.

TURNIP PURÉE

2 pounds white turnips with fresh green tops	Salt
1 cube butter	Grated white pepper
Cream	Ground nutmeg

1. Scrub the turnips and then peel. Cut into pieces. In a saucepan, melt the butter and steam the turnips, covered, over low heat for 45 minutes. When done, they should be very soft when tested with a fork. Drain well and force through a fine sieve.

2. Return the purée to the heat and cook out all the excess moisture, stirring constantly to avoid burning. Add enough cream to give it the consistency of mashed potatoes and if more of a butter taste is desired, add some of the butter the turnips were cooked in.

3. Put in pastry bag and decorate rim of dinner plates. Place tournedos in the center.
   Turnips are at their peak in the fall, but are available all year around. Try to get young ones which are firm and heavy.

The context that makes a restaurant great simply cannot be defined. You have to create an environment for yourself to function out of that's bigger than all your positions in life. . . that gives people the opportunity to be brilliant.

SALAD OF SEASONAL GREENS

Bibb lettuce	*Purslane*
Nasturtium leaves	*VINAIGRETTE*
Lamb's quarter greens	*Nasturtium flowers*
Dandelion greens	*Borage flowers*

Wash all greens thoroughly; drain, dry and chill. At serving time, break up or tear the greens and combine in a salad bowl. Toss greens with Vinaigrette until leaves are coated. Garnish with the 2 types of flowers.

VINAIGRETTE

¼ *cup walnut oil*	*Salt*
½ *cup white chicken stock*	*Pepper*
¼ *cup white wine vinegar*	

Combine all ingredients in a jar and shake.

Fresh herbs are a nice addition with the greens, such as fresh basil.

The Other Place may have more access than most people to unusual greens grown by our local farmers, but you will be surprised how much is available in several health food stores or the Pike Place Market to create exciting new salads at home. Growing greens in your own kitchen garden can also be a year-round constant delight.

THE OTHER PLACE

BLUEBERRY TART

TOPPING:
- 2 cups water
- 1 cup sugar
- 2 boxes blueberries, cleaned
  Small jar currant jelly

CRUST:
- 1½ cups pastry flour
- ½ teaspoon salt
- ⅓ cup sugar
- 9 ounces cold unsalted butter
- 1 egg plus 1 yolk

CREAM FILLING:
- 2 cups milk
- 1 vanilla bean
- 6 egg yolks
- ⅔ cup sugar
- ½ cup flour
- 2 tablespoons liqueur, such as Kirsch or brandy

1. To make the Crust, mix together flour, salt and sugar. Cut in cold butter. Beat in egg and yolk just until mixture holds together. Line a 9-inch flan ring with the pastry. Prick with a fork. Weight with waxed paper and beans. Bake at 350° for approximately 45 minutes or until golden brown and completely cooked. Cool.

2. To make the Cream Filling, bring milk and vanilla bean to a boil. Remove from heat and take out vanilla bean. Beat egg yolk and sugar with a wire whisk until thick and light. Add flour and continue whisking. Slowly add hot milk, beating constantly.

3. To make Topping, bring water and sugar to a boil and boil rapidly for 5 minutes. Reduce heat and poach blueberries in syrup, being sure not to let syrup go above a simmer. You do not want blueberries to burst. Cool berries in the syrup.

4. For the final preparation, drain the cooled berries through a sieve and spread over the filling. Melt current jelly and pour over the berries for a glaze.

It is best to put all three parts together just before serving. Do not assemble this the day before. Each of the three parts can be made ahead of time, but you

should assemble the tart no more than two hours before serving or the crust will become soggy. If you are making the cream ahead, cover it with waxed paper pressed onto the surface to avoid the formation of a "skin" on top.

The Palm Court

Dinner for Four

Clams Simmered in White Wine

Cream of Snapper with Mint

Dungeness Crab Legs and Spinach with Raspberry Vinegar Dressing

Veal Medallions with Celery and Madagascar Sauce

Grand Marnier Soufflé

Wine:

With Crab Legs—Joseph Phelps Fumé Blanc

With Veal—Clos DuBois Chardonnay,
or
Château Croizet-Bages, Haut-Médoc

Westin Hotel, Owner

Harold White, Manager

Dennis Kolodziejski, Executive Chef, Westin Hotel

Michel Soulet, Palm Court Chef

There is probably no restaurant in Seattle more elegant or more sumptuous in decor than the Palm Court, located on the lobby level of the Westin Hotel. Everywhere are mirrors, magnificent crystal chandeliers, and huge potted palms in brass planters. More than half the seating is in the glass atrium, called the Pavilion, which is illuminated at night by a heaven of Tivoli lights. The remaining seating is in comfortably upholstered banquettes lining the upper tier of the room. Persimmon, rust, and taupe color the rich fabric of the brocaded walls, the high-backed upholstered chairs, and the patterned carpeting. Baby orchids in cut crystal vases adorn each table. Only fine china, crystal, and silver are used at each place setting.

A beautiful marble, glass, and brass staircase leads up to Shampers, the English colloquial expression meaning champagne, where large parties of 14 to 32 can enjoy the luxury of a private dining room. Shampers boasts its own lovely bar and reception area, and echos the formal dining atmosphere of the Palm Court it overlooks.

The Palm Court opened in October, 1981, with the goal "to set a new standard for dining in Seattle." A primary objective of the restaurant is to excel in continental and fresh regional cuisine, a trend toward using fresh ingredients and an artistic presentation. Although the emphasis is on basic food, the end result is both exciting and innovative at the weekday lunches and at the nightly dinners.

Under the direction of executive chef Dennis Kolodziejski, who came to Seattle directly from the Westin Hotel restaurant in Cincinnati, Ohio, each meal is cooked with special care and with only the freshest and tastiest ingredients, some of which are regularly imported from around the world.

Since the day it opened, the Palm Court has been dedicated to excellence. Its accomplishment to this end is clear, for the Palm Court has been selected as a Travel/Holiday Award winning restaurant for the past three years, and just this year received the prestigious Ambassador 25 Award and an excellence honor for its wine list. There is a very obvious pride and enthusiasm among the staff as they strive to make the Palm Court "first and best in food and service."

1900 5th Avenue

CLAMS SIMMERED IN WHITE WINE

¼ cup FISH FUMET
   or stock
½ cup white wine
1 cup brunoise of carrots,
   celery, leek, and onion
2 dozen butter clams,
   thoroughly washed

¾ cup heavy cream
Salt and pepper to taste
Chopped parsley
French bread

1. Combine the Fumet or stock, wine, and brunoise in a pan with a tight-fitting cover over high heat. Add the clams, cover, and steam 2 to 4 minutes or until all the clams have opened. (Discard any that will not open.)
2. Remove the clams from the broth and remove the shells. Place the meats in four soup plates.
3. Add the cream to the broth; reduce over medium heat until thickened to a very light sauce consistency. Season to taste with salt and pepper.
4. Pour the sauce over the clams. Sprinkle with parsley and serve with French bread.

Note: A *brunoise* is a very finely diced combination of vegetables, normally including carrot, onion, and celery, used to flavor a broth and give it body.

Mussels are equally wonderful when used in place of clams in this recipe.

FISH FUMET

2 pounds halibut bones
1 carrot, sliced
1 leek, sliced
1 stalk celery, sliced

1 bay leaf
1 sprig fresh thyme
1 sprig fresh rosemary
4 tablespoons butter

1. Place the fish bones, vegetables, herbs, and butter in a stock pot over low heat. Cover and cook, stirring occasionally, until the vegetables are tender.
2. Add water just to cover. Simmer 30 minutes.
3. Strain the broth into another pot, reserving the herbs and discarding the vegetables. Return the broth to medium heat and cook until reduced to 1 cup.

CREAM OF SNAPPER WITH MINT

1 cup brunoise of celery,
   carrot, and leek
4 tablespoons butter
¼ cup flour
3 cups FISH FUMET
   (see previous page)

½ cup white wine
½ pound red snapper, diced
2 teaspoons chopped mint
½ cup heavy cream
½ cup whipped cream

1. Sauté the brunoise in the butter in a heavy saucepan. When tender, stir in the flour and cook briefly. Do not allow to brown.
2. Add the Fish Fumet gradually, stirring constantly. Return to a boil and stir in the wine.
3. Add the snapper and cook just long enough to cook through. Be careful not to overcook or the fish will crumble.
4. Add the mint and heavy cream just before serving.
5. Ladle the soup into individual bowls. Serve with a dollop of whipped cream on each.

Being in the Northwest, which has an abundance of fish, we enjoy preparing and serving this recipe.

DUNGENESS CRAB LEGS AND SPINACH WITH RASPBERRY VINEGAR DRESSING

2 cups fresh spinach leaves
32 mint leaves
16 Dungeness crab legs

RASPBERRY VINEGAR DRESSING

1. Carefully wash and dry the spinach leaves. Tear into bite-size pieces.
2. Tear the mint leaves, and then toss the mint with the spinach.
3. Place a handful of the greens on each salad plate. Arrange four crab legs apiece on top of the greens and drizzle with Raspberry Vinegar Dressing to taste.

RASPBERRY VINEGAR DRESSING

½ cup raspberry vinegar
¾ cup salad oil
1 tablespoon chopped shallots

Salt and pepper to taste
Pinch of sugar (optional)

Blend all ingredients thoroughly. If the dressing is too sour, a little sugar may be added.

This is an exotic combination of flavors: the mint with the spinach is very provocative.

VEAL MEDALLIONS WITH CELERY AND MADAGASCAR SAUCE

8 (2-ounce) veal medallions
¼ cup flour
6 tablespoons oil
Salt and pepper to taste
1 celery root
¼ pound butter
1 medium-size carrot, finely diced

½ medium-size onion, finely diced
8 mushrooms, sliced
1 teaspoon pink peppercorns
¾ cup white wine
¾ cup fresh cream or heavy cream
Lemon juice to taste

1. Dust the veal medallions with flour.
2. Heat the oil in a skillet and brown the medallions on each side. Remove from the pan; season with salt and pepper to taste and keep warm.
3. Cut the celery root in half. Finely dice one half; julienne the other half and reserve.
4. Pour off most of the oil from the skillet. Add 4 tablespoons of the butter to the same skillet. Add the diced vegetables and mushrooms and sauté for 1 minute.
5. Add the peppercorns and the white wine; continue cooking until the sauce is reduced by half.
6. Add the cream, bring to a boil, and continue boiling until the sauce is smooth. Season with salt, pepper, and lemon juice. Stir in the remaining butter.
7. Serve the veal medallions on beds of julienned celery root, coated with sauce.

At The Palm Court we serve two fresh vegetables with lunch and three fresh vegetables with dinner. We no longer serve a starch routinely.

GRAND MARNIER SOUFFLÉ

2 cups milk
½ cup plus 1 tablespoon sugar
½ cup butter
½ cup flour
8 egg yolks
2 tablespoons vanilla
 extract

6 tablespoons Grand
 Marnier liqueur
4 egg whites
SAUCE

1. Preheat oven to 350°.
2. Bring the milk, sugar, and butter to a boil in a saucepan. As soon as the mixture boils, remove from heat and add the flour all at once. Stir in well. Allow to cool for a few minutes.
3. Add the egg yolks one at a time, stirring well after each addition. Stir in the vanilla extract and Grand Marnier.
4. Beat the egg whites to stiff peaks. Fold in 2 cups of the yolk mixture, discarding any remainder.
5. Divide the batter among four 5-ounce soufflé dishes. Bake in pre-heated oven for 20 minutes. Prepare the Sauce while the soufflés are baking.
6. Serve immediately upon removing from the oven, with the Sauce on the side.

To make a wonderful Chocolate Soufflé, use the same recipe but omit the Grand Marnier; add 9 ounces melted chocolate and use 5 egg whites instead of 4.

SAUCE

2 egg yolks
½ cup heavy cream

1 teaspoon powdered sugar

Beat the egg yolks, then beat in the cream and powdered sugar.

PETIT CAFÉ

✠✠✠✠

Dinner for Four

Kir Vermouth

Escargots au Roquefort

Poulet à la Moutarde

Mousse de Poireaux

Navarin de Mouton

Salade Petit Café

Poires Belle-Hélène

Wine:

*With Escargot and Poulet—Mâcon Lugny,
Les Charmes, 1983*

With Navarin—Vosne-Romanée, 1977 or 1978

Remy Newland and Bryce Robinson, Owners

Abdul Muhalhal, Chef

At just half a block up the street from the original site of the intimate French bistro, Le Petit Cafe is now doubled in space and elegance. One glimpse at the blue sidewalk awning and sheer white curtains from the outside provides a taste of the all-so-French ambiance within, with its high open ceilings, dusty-blue walls, enormous, sweet bouquets, tear-drop chandeliers and French paintings. Le Petit Cafe is somewhat of a Versailles in Seattle.

The blue menu is also fit for royalty. After difficult choices among apéritifs, champagnes and sauternes, guests are tempted with hot or cold hors d'oeuvres, among which the fabulous crab mousse, in the opinion of co-owner Remy Newland, is a "not to be missed" item. One is eventually subjected to the ritual of the entrée choice, where a variety of tantalizing Algerian couscous grains including chicken, homemade Algerian sausage and lamb, are still the speciality of the house. A certain melt-in-the-mouth scallop dish, featuring large scallops flown in from the Mediterranean, prepared in a creamy, buttery champagne sauce and garnished with mushrooms and baby shrimp in a puffy pastry shell, is also an old favorite which speaks for itself. And if the customer is still willing and capable, a fresh dessert tray is then waved before his eyes.

Strangely enough, all this and more are created by a man with a mathematics degree from the University of Washington. Abdul Muhalhal, who grew up in Libya and there learned cooking from his mother while working in their family-owned restaurant, finds being a chef a "very satisfying way to make a living." Abdul is quite obviously good at what he does, and Remy likes to refer to him as "one of the young, creative geniuses in town."

The European elegance of the 50-seat cafe is offset by a quaint casualness, particularly evident in the front room where an assortment of adorable stuffed German teddy bears lines the walls. These collectables, in addition to numerous toy soldiers, cars and knickknacks, are vestiges of Bryce Robinson's former days as an antique merchant, and add a comfortable charm to the French dining atmosphere.

Le Petit Cafe believes in carefully prepared French and North African cuisine and a rich and pleasant environment; but it does not subscribe to poshness. "We don't consider ourselves really fancy," explains Remy "We are simply a friendly place."

3428 Northeast 55th Street

LE PETIT CAFÉ

KIR VERMOUTH

Per Serving:

1 ounce crème de cassis	Lemon twist
4 to 5 ounces dry white vermouth, chilled	

Measure the crème de cassis into each glass. Fill with the vermouth and add the twist of lemon. Serve with or without ice.

ESCARGOTS AU ROQUEFORT

¼ pound butter	White pepper
3 ounces Roquefort cheese	1 tablespoon brandy
1 teaspoon dried tarragon, or 1 tablespoon fresh	24 snails
	¼ cup bread crumbs
1 teaspoon dried chervil, or 1 tablespoon fresh	French bread

1. Preheat broiler.
2. Place the butter, Roquefort, herbs, pepper and brandy in a food processor fitted with a steel blade. Process the mixture until thoroughly blended to a paste.
3. Melt the paste in a skillet over low heat—do not boil. Once the paste is melted, add the snails. Stir constantly until heated through.
4. Place six snails on each of four dishes or escargot platters. Divide the sauce evenly over the snails. Sprinkle the bread crumbs over and place under preheated broiler until golden brown, about 2 minutes. Serve with fresh French bread.

NAVARIN DE MOUTON

3 carrots
4 tablespoons butter
2 teaspoons vegetable
  or olive oil
2 onions, coarsely chopped
2 pounds boneless leg
  of lamb, cleaned and
  cut in 1½" cubes
½ cup flour
1 head garlic
1 leek, white only, halved
4 sprigs parsley, stems
  included

2 bay leaves
1 stalk celery
3 fresh tomatoes, diced
1 teaspoon thyme
  Salt and pepper
1 cup dry white wine,
  plus more as needed
1 pound turnips, peeled
  and cubed
1 pound baby red potatoes,
  scrubbed

1. Preheat oven to 400°.
2. Slice two of the carrots into circles about ⅛ inch thick. Cut the other carrot in half and reserve for the bouquet garni.
3. Melt the butter with the oil in a large ovenproof skillet over moderately high heat. Add the sliced carrots and chopped onions and sauté for 3 to 4 minutes or until the vegetables have softened but not browned.
4. Add the lamb; brown the meat on all sides. Drain off the excess grease and sprinkle the flour over the pan. Toss to coat the meat and vegetables.
5. Bury the whole garlic head in the mixture. Tie together the reserved carrot, leek, parsley sprigs, bay leaves, and celery with a piece of string and bury the bundle in the mixture. Add the diced tomatoes, thyme, and salt and pepper to taste.
6. Add 2 cups water and the wine. The liquid should just cover the meat; if it does not, add more wine. Place the turnips together on one side of the pan.
7. Cover and bake in preheated oven for 1 hour.
8. Place the baby potatoes together on another side of the pan; re-cover

and continue to bake for another 30 minutes or until everything is fork-tender.

9. Remove and discard the garlic and bouquet garni. Remove the turnips and potatoes separately with a slotted spoon. If you wish to strain the pan sauce, remove the meat with a slotted spoon and pour the sauce through a strainer. Serve the lamb, carrots, and onion with plenty of pan sauce and the turnips and potatoes on the side.

Many butchers will be glad to bone a leg of lamb for you. Remove as much fat and connective tissue as possible before cutting the meat into cubes.

SALADE PETIT CAFÉ

3 tablespoons red wine vinegar	1 egg yolk
	Salt and pepper
1 teaspoon chopped garlic	⅔ cup olive oil or vegetable
½ to 1 teaspoon tarragon	oil (or a combination)
2 tablespoons Dijon-style mustard	1 head red leaf lettuce, rinsed and thoroughly dried

1. Place the first six ingredients in a small bowl. Whisk together.

2. Gradually whisk in the oil. If the mixture is too thick, add a little cold water or more vinegar. If it is too thin, add more oil. Taste and adjust the seasoning.

3. Pour onto the dried greens and toss gently but thoroughly.

POULET A LA MOUTARDE

¼ pound plus 1 tablespoon
   butter
2 tablespoons vegetable oil
4 (8-ounce) boned and
   skinned chicken breasts
3 tablespoons cognac
¼ cup minced shallots
3 tablespoons Dijon-style
   mustard

1 cup dry white wine
   Salt and pepper
1 egg yolk
1 teaspoon lemon juice
   (more or less to taste)
1 cup heavy cream

1. In a stainless steel or enameled skillet, melt ¼ pound butter and the oil over moderately high heat. Add the chicken breasts and cook until lightly browned. Remove the chicken to a platter and cover with foil to keep warm.

2. Heat the cognac in the same skillet. Ignite with a match, stirring until the flame dies.

3. Add the remaining 1 tablespoon butter to the pan, allow to melt, and add the minced shallots. Cook, stirring frequently, until lightly browned.

4. Return the chicken to the pan. Combine the mustard and wine and pour the mixture over the chicken. Add salt and pepper to taste. Cover and let simmer until the breasts are resilient when touched and fork-tender, about 15 to 20 minutes. Overcooking will produce a tough, dry dish.

5. Separately, mix the egg yolk, lemon juice, and cream together in a small bowl. Pour the mixture over the breasts in the skillet. Stir this mixture into any liquid that has formed in the skillet and toss the breasts to coat thoroughly. Without boiling, continue to cook for 1 to 2 minutes.

6. Place the breasts on individual heated serving plates and spoon the sauce evenly over each. Serve with Mousse de Poireaux.

MOUSSE DE POIREAUX
Leek Mousse

3 pounds whole, young leeks	Salt and freshly ground pepper
6 tablespoons butter	1 cup heavy cream

1. Remove most of the green stalks from the leeks, leaving only a hint of green near the white portion, if it is tender. Cut lengthwise into fourths and wash very well, removing any grit that may be trapped between the rings. Dry well with paper towels. Chop to a medium dice.
2. Over medium heat, melt 4 tablespoons of the butter in a skillet. When the butter has completely melted and the foam begins to subside, add the chopped leek. Cook about 30 minutes or until soft but not browned, stirring frequently. Add salt and pepper to taste.
3. Transfer the leeks to a food processor fitted with a steel blade. Process for 4 minutes.
4. With the motor running, add the cream through the feed tube and process 1 more minute.
5. Heat the remaining 2 tablespoons butter in a small pan and, after it melts and is slightly brown, pour the butter into the mousse mixture in the processor. Mix well. Taste for salt and pepper, adding more as needed.
6. Keep the mixture warm in a bain marie until ready to serve.

POIRES BELLE-HÉLÈNE

2 quarts medium-strength Earl Grey tea	1 cup heavy cream
2 firm pears (preferably d'Anjou)	1 teaspoon vanilla extract
1 lemon, halved	2 teaspoons confectioners' sugar
2 cups chocolate sauce	8 small scoops vanilla ice cream
2 tablespoons triple sec liqueur	

1. Bring the tea to a simmer in an enameled or stainless-steel saucepan over medium heat.

2. Cut each pear in half. Peel, core, and immediately rub the surface with the lemon.

3. Place the pear halves in the hot tea and poach for 3 to 4 minutes on each side, or until tender but still firm. Some varieties of pear will poach faster than others, so keep an eye on them. Remove from the tea with a slotted spoon and set aside to cool.

4. In a separate saucepan, slowly heat the chocolate sauce. Stir in the triple sec; keep warm.

5. Whip the heavy cream to soft peaks. Add the vanilla extract and confectioners' sugar and whip to stiff peaks.

6. Place one pear half on each of four cold serving plates, hollowed side up. Place two scoops of ice cream on each pear half. Drizzle each pear with ½ cup of the heated chocolate sauce (or to taste) and immediately top with a generous dollop of whipped cream.

ray's boathouse

Dinner for Six

Shrimp-Stuffed Artichokes

Ray's Boathouse Salad

Teriyaki Salmon

Glazed Carrots

Ray's Cheesecake

Wine:

With Appetizer—Hinzerling White Riesling, 1983

With Salad—Ste. Michelle Fumé Blanc, 1983

With Entrée—Trefethen Vineyards Chardonnay, 1982

With Dessert—Château Rieussec Sauternes, 1979

Russ Wohlers, Earl Lasher and Elizabeth Ginrich, Owners

Wayne Ludvigsen, Kitchen Manager

Karl Zimmer, Assistant Kitchen Manager

"**R**ay's Boathouse has to have the best location in the state of Washington. It couldn't be a better reflection of the things Seattle is. It is marine oriented: it is water and light. It has a panoramic outlook of Bainbridge Island and the Olympic Mountains. Each year from our windows we can see sunsets move north from West Point to Port Madison as the summer progresses." Ric Prideaux, general manager of Ray's Boathouse, here clearly confirms the common opinion of countless others: "Our view is one of the most outstanding features of our restaurant." Built on pilings in the waters of the Shilshole Bay and dominated by expansive lengths of large windows, Ray's Boathouse often seems to be floating in the Puget Sound.

When the owners of Ray's purchased the landmark restaurant in 1973, they decided to devote themselves to being a dinner house. "The most important aspect of our business is our kitchen and the food that comes out of it," says Ric. "We serve quality Northwest seafood at reasonable prices. The menu is not complex, but the items offered are distinctive and top quality. Our salmon, for example, is cooked naturally over mesquite charcoal. We buy the finest quality fresh fish available, whether it be oysters, sole, halibut, black cod or albacore.

"Of course, we always serve fresh vegetables and fruits, and the soups and desserts are made right here daily. Our wine list has grown tremendously in the past few years, focusing particularly on the finest quality Northwest wines."

In May, 1984, Ray's owners established a second restaurant in downtown Seattle. While the dining environment is a bit more formal with its glass and marble touches, the city center Ray's makes use of the same menu, style, and staff. "It is packaged in a more modern building, but the philosophy remains the same."

The decor of Ray's is casual and unobtrusive; nothing should detract from the view. Over each wooden table at the windows and over each more secluded booth is a hanging copper lamp, hand made by Julie Speidel. A painting by a Northwest artist is on the wall of each booth, and the real-life water scene surrounds each table. It is a comfortable and beautiful setting for dining where the food is always predictably good.

6049 Seaview Avenue Northwest
2nd and Marion

SHRIMP-STUFFED ARTICHOKES

6 artichokes
1 pound cream cheese
1 teaspoon tarragon
1 teaspoon sweet basil
½ teaspoon celery salt
2 teaspoons lemon juice
1 tablespoon Worcester-
    shire sauce

1 tablespoon minced onion
2 tablespoons minced celery
1 tablespoon grated
    Parmesan cheese
1¾ cups mayonnaise
1½ cups shrimp, more or less
    may be used according
    to taste
Parsley for decoration

1. Remove stem and top leaves from artichokes. Steam for about 45 minutes. Allow to cool.
2. Meanwhile, add all remaining ingredients except shrimp and parsley and set aside.
3. Remove the centers from the artichokes and fill with cheese mixture.
4. Top with shrimp and a sprig of parsley. Serve chilled.

Ray's Boathouse is open seven nights a week all year long, with the exception of Thanksgiving, Christmas Eve, Christmas Day, and June 25, which is the annual employee picnic.

RAY'S BOATHOUSE SALAD

½ head Bibb lettuce
½ bunch spinach

½ head romaine
3 ounces blue cheese

1. Thoroughly wash the lettuce, spinach and romaine. Cut or tear the greens into bite-size pieces.
2. Toss with crumbled blue cheese and Dressing.

DRESSING

2 ounces Dijon mustard
1 ounce olive oil
1 teaspoon salt
1 tablespoon coarsely
   ground pepper

1 tablespoon ground
   oregano
2 ounces apple cider vinegar
4 ounces salad oil

Mix all ingredients except the vinegar and the salad oil. Slowly add vinegar, while continuing to mix. Finally, add the salad oil very slowly, mixing constantly.

TERIYAKI SALMON

1 quart soy sauce
1 pound brown sugar
1 teaspoon dry mustard
2 freshly crushed garlic
   cloves
1 tablespoon chopped fresh
   ginger

½ cup white wine
6 salmon filets, about
   8 ounces each
   Toasted sesame seeds

1. Prepare the marinade by combining all ingredients except salmon and sesame seeds.
2. Place filets in the teriyaki marinade and allow to marinate 4 to 6 hours.
3. Broil the salmon on a grill until done, about 7 to 10 minutes. Top with toasted sesame seeds.

GLAZED CARROTS

24 small carrots (skin on)
5 ounces butter

3 ounces brown sugar
1 tablespoon dill weed

1. Steam the carrots for 5 to 6 minutes.

2. Combine the butter, brown sugar and dill weed. Glaze the cooked carrots with this mixture.

RAY'S CHEESECAKE

Graham cracker crumbs	*4 large eggs*
2 pounds cream cheese	*TOPPING*
1 cup sugar	*Walnut granules for garnish*
1 tablespoon vanilla	

1. Coat the bottom of a 9-inch spring-form pan with a very thin layer of graham cracker crumbs.
2. Cream together the cream cheese, sugar, vanilla and eggs. Pour into spring-form pan.
3. Bake at 325° for about 45 minutes, or until the top begins to crack. Take out of the oven and allow to cool for 30 minutes on a rack—air circulation is essential.
4. Pour Topping over cake, spreading evenly. Bake for 10 minutes at 425°. Allow to cool slightly. Top with walnut granules and chill.

TOPPING

2 cups sour cream	*1 tablespoon vanilla*
3 tablespoons sugar	

Mix all ingredients well.

The three owners of Ray's Boathouse also own Ray's Oasis Restaurant in Boise, Idaho, and Ray's Seafood Restaurant in the Waikiki Shopping Plaza in Honolulu, Hawaii. All of the restaurants strive to serve distinctive and fresh food at reasonable prices.

Settebello

Dinner for Six

Calamaretti Ripieni al Forno

Rigatoni con Prosciutto, Pomodoro, e Cipolla

Scaloppini di Vitello al Vino Marsala e Funghi Freschi

Insalata Fresca di Stagione

Zabaglione al Gusto Frangelico

Beverages:

With Squid and Pasta—Pinot Grìgio del Trentino

With Veal and Salad—Barolo or Chianti Clàssico

With Zabaglione—Vin Santo di Toscana

After Dinner—espresso coffee

Luciano Bardinelli, Owner and Chef

SETTEBELLO

Located in a curving, wedge-shaped building overlooking one of Seattle's more interesting city blocks, Settebello displays the modern Italian flair for design. Split levels and low partitions divide the space into a pleasant maze of functional units. Splashes of color and an occasional natural wood finish against the background of greyish shades create a clean, vital atmosphere to complement the cuisine. Along one wall, a narrow kitchen produces the zesty Northern Italian specialties for which the restaurant, in the mere three years since it opened, has become famous.

"We strive to use the best produce, the best materials," says owner Luciano Bardinelli. "Each item that we use has its own flavor; we try to bring that out in the preparation. The secret of any good food is to keep it simple—if your materials are good, of course. We produce—at least we think we do—the best that Italian cuisine has to offer."

Although Settebello's success has been instant, Bardinelli reminds us that it is the culmination of 20 years of experience with restaurants. Born in Milan, he entered the business at 16. After a period in Switzerland, "where I learned to make Steak Tartare the right way," he came to the United States. Before opening Settebello, he worked in Los Angeles, Las Vegas, and San Francisco as maître d', manager, and owner. "I've worked mostly out front. Of course, I cook—I have a lot of love for food and a lot of love for what I do in front."

"The difficulty in opening Settebello was in not knowing how the public here would like what we offer," he says. "I opened a similar restaurant in San Francisco a while back and it was well received, but you never know what will happen. It's worked very well, though. People here are more appreciative, more sincere in their response to what we do. The people that come here go and tell the chef or the manager that they had a good meal and they enjoyed it. That kind of response escaped me in San Francisco."

Settebello's simplicity and goodness, straight from the northernmost part of Italy, is indeed happily received in Seattle.

1525 East Olive Way

CALAMARETTI RIPIENI AL FORNO

12 small squid	Bread crumbs
1 clove garlic	¼ cup olive oil
¼ bunch fresh parsley,	Salt and pepper
chopped (approximately)	½ cup dry white wine

1. Preheat oven to 350°.

2. To clean the squid, remove the cartilage, the black ink sac, and the yellow beak under the head. Rinse in plenty of cold water. Dry with a towel.

3. Detach the tentacles from the "sails." Chop the tentacles with the garlic and parsley, then mix with bread crumbs to taste and enough olive oil to moisten. Season to taste with salt and pepper.

4. Fill the sails with the chopped mixture. Close with toothpicks.

5. Place the remaining olive oil in an ovenproof sauté pan over high heat. When the oil is hot, add the stuffed squid. Moisten with the oil in the pan and season lightly with salt and pepper. Add the wine and place in preheated oven for 12 minutes or until done. Remove the toothpicks and serve immediately.

The secret of any good food is to keep it as simple as you can; and, of course, to use the best materials. You want to give each item a chance to develop its individual flavor.

RIGATONI CON PROSCIUTTO, POMODORO, E CIPOLLA

2 pounds Italian pear	Salt
tomatoes (preferably fresh)	2 pounds rigatoni pasta
2 tablespoons olive oil	(preferably imported)
¼ onion, finely chopped	¼ pound Parmesan cheese,
Pinch of crushed red pepper	freshly grated
½ pound prosciutto ham,	
cut in small julienne	

1. If using fresh tomatoes, cut the stem ends out and place in boiling water for about 1 minute to loosen the skins; remove and peel. Cut in julienne and drain well.
2. Bring at least 6 quarts salted water to a rolling boil.
3. Meanwhile, heat the olive oil in a sauté pan over high heat. Add the onion, red pepper, and prosciutto and sauté until the onion becomes lightly golden. Add the tomatoes and salt to taste. Reduce heat and simmer for 8 to 10 minutes.
4. Add the rigatoni to the rapidly boiling water a little at a time to maintain a rolling boil, but not excessively slowly. Cook al dente, stirring occasionally. Drain and place in a large bowl.
5. Pour the sauce over the pasta. Add the grated cheese, mix well, and serve.

If you are using fresh tomatoes, you will try not to overpower their flavor with a lot of spices—you want the freshness to come through.

SCALOPPINI DI VITELLO AL VINO MARSALA E FUNGHI FRESCHI

18 (1½- to 2-ounce) scaloppini of veal loin
Salt and pepper
Flour for dredging

¾ pound butter
2 cups Marsala wine
1 pound fresh mushrooms, sliced

1. Season the veal with salt and pepper and then dredge very lightly in flour.
2. Melt ½ pound butter in a very large sauté pan over low heat. Add the veal; raise the heat to high and sauté on both sides until golden.
3. Add the Marsala and allow to reduce by four-fifths, still over high heat. Remove the veal to a heated serving plate.
4. Add 1 tablespoon water and the remaining ¼ pound butter to the

pan. When hot, add the sliced mushrooms and sauté rapidly for 1 to 2 minutes. Cover the scaloppini with the sauce and serve immediately.

Note: If you don't have a pan large enough to hold all the scaloppini in one layer, you may cook the veal in stages, adding butter as needed.

INSALATINA FRESCA DI STAGIONE

3 *heads soft-textured*
  lettuce in season
2 *pinches salt*
1 *pinch black pepper*

1 *tablespoon red wine*
  vinegar
3 *tablespoons olive oil*

Wash the lettuce and dry well. Tear into large pieces and place in a salad bowl. Add the salt and pepper, then the vinegar and oil. Toss lightly and serve.

Bibb lettuce or endive are examples of greens for this salad.

ZABAGLIONE AL GUSTO FRANGELICO

12 *eggs, separated*
 6 *tablespoons sugar*

¼ *cup Frangelico liqueur*

1. In the top of a large double boiler, beat the egg whites until stiff.
2. Add the egg yolks and sugar, place over boiling water, beating constantly until firm enough that the whisk leaves a ribbon lasting a few seconds on the surface of the mixture.
3. Add the Frangelico and continue to beat until the mixture has the consistency of a soft custard. Take care not to overcook; the eggs will scramble if cooked too long. Serve immediately.

the surrogate hostess

Dinner for Six

Chicken Liver-Mushroom Pâté

Mediterranean Salad

Spinach Noodles with Ricotta-Walnut Sauce

Crème Caramel

Wine:

With Pâté—Château Camus Graves, 1976

With Pasta—Travaligni Gattinara, 1973

Sean Seedlock, Owner

Vicky McCraffree, Kitchen Manager

After over five years of working his way up through the ranks at The Surrogate Hostess, present owner Sean Seedlock can honestly say that he knows his restaurant from the inside out. Starting with the in-house bakery on the premises, then progressing to bakery manager and eventually general manager, Sean purchased the restaurant from its previous owner nearly one and a half years ago. The philosophy under which he was trained at The Surrogate Hostess is still one of his restaurant's strong holds today: "We are always dealing with the freshest and finest of ingredients, which our chefs carefully select and painstakingly prepare daily."

The Surrogate Hostess is not an ordinary restaurant. The decor is functional. Everyone sits together at long wooden tables, and there is a large working kitchen which is kept immaculate. No smoking is allowed. A changing variety of wines is available by the glass or by the bottle.

Although the bright cafeteria-style atmosphere at the Surrogate Hostess has remained straightforward and consistent throughout the years, a new emphasis in cooking concepts has emerged. The chefs have gradually progressed to a more pronounced usage of spices and seasonings, which lends to the cuisine a very particular and memorable accent. Evening meals have consequently become more complex, and as the dinner trade at the Surrogate Hostess has expanded, chefs are now also cooking to order.

The newly flavored dishes are offered on a menu which receives considerable renovation four times a year; in addition there are regular specialty items. The Surrogate Hostess is based on what Sean calls a "constant variety;" within the numerous seasonal changes there is a strong "continuity and consistency which keeps our guests coming back for more. We have a very loyal clientele, which shows that we are providing a real, honest, quality product."

In addition to the renowned, aromatic bakery on location, the Surrogate Hostess also boasts an extensive catering service. "We gladly cater in-home breakfasts, wedding receptions, corporate accounts, and everything inbetween." As with all things Sean and his crew set their hands to, here again it is the consistency of high quality which keeps the Surrogate Hostess in the ranks of Seattle's superior dining establishments.

746 19th Avenue East

CHICKEN LIVER-MUSHROOM PÂTE

1 cup unsalted butter
2 pounds chicken livers, trimmed
½ pound sliced mushrooms
½ cup chopped parsley

½ cup minced shallots
1 teaspoon whole thyme
1 teaspoon salt
⅓ cup brandy
¼ cup clarified butter

1. Melt butter in large sauté pan. Add all ingredients except the brandy and clarified butter. Cook over medium heat until livers are just firm but still slightly pink in the center.
2. Warm brandy and ignite. Pour over liver mixture and shake pan until flame dies. Let cool to room temperature.
3. Purée in blender in several batches. Pour into one large mold or several small ones. Top with clarified butter. Refrigerate.

The key point with anything made with chicken livers is to not overcook the livers. They should be slightly pink in the center when you cut into them.

We have developed this variation of the chicken liver pâté. This particular one is a combination of flavors we think is very good. Actually, all you're looking for in any pâté is the flavor. It's very easy to make substitutions: for example, any favorite wine can be used instead of the brandy.

MEDITERRANEAN SALAD

2 to 3 pounds tomatoes
1 tablespoon dry Greek oregano
3 cucumbers
¼ cup freshly minced parsley
1 red onion, thinly sliced

1 cup black olives
½ pound feta cheese, crumbled
Coarse black pepper to taste
VINAIGRETTE DRESSING

1. Cut tomatoes into wedges and place in a collander to drain. Sprinkle with oregano.

2. Peel cucumbers and cut in half lengthwise. Remove seeds and slice into crescent shapes.

3. Combine all ingredients and toss lightly with *VINAIGRETTE SAUCE.*

VINAIGRETTE DRESSING

1 teaspoon Dijon mustard
1 teaspoon salt
1 clove garlic, mashed
2 tablespoons red wine
   vinegar

6 tablespoons olive oil
Large pinch black pepper

Blend mustard, salt, garlic and vinegar into a paste and whisk olive oil in, drop by drop, until emulsified. Add pepper to taste.

We use vinaigrettes for all of our dressings because we are serving the vegetables and not the dressing. Other dressings are fine, but anything you dress with a heavy dressing becomes the dressing. A vinaigrette enhances rather than overwhelms the flavor of the salad.

SPINACH NOODLES WITH RICOTTA-WALNUT SAUCE

1¾ cups ricotta cheese
½ cup heavy cream
½ cup minced walnuts
1 tablespoon oregano

1¼ cups Madiera
3 pounds spinach noodles
   Grated Parmesan cheese
   Minced parsley

1. Mix ricotta cheese with heavy cream and add walnuts. Soak basil and oregano in Madiera. Combine the two mixtures and heat in a bain marie.

2. Cook spinach noodles in rapidly boiling salted water approximately 5 minutes, or until al dente. Drain.

3. Toss hot noodles with cheese sauce and spoon into warm soup plates. Garnish with a generous toss of Parmesan and a teaspoon or so of finely minced parsley.

Use a high quality, preferably fresh pasta if you don't make your own. Fresh pasta is available at De Laurenti's and La Coppa Pan in the Public Market. If you are buying off the shelf, be sure you buy a pasta with at least 50% Semolina flour. Semolina is a gutsier type of grain than the usual wheat variety. Remember that fresh pasta cooks in sometime one-third the time of the supermarket noodles. Pasta is done when it is al dente—still slightly chewy.

A bain marie is a water bath, a pan of water in which is set a smaller pan containing the food to be heated.

CRÈME CARMEL

1 cup granulated sugar	1 vanilla bean
2 tablespoons water	3 eggs
2½ cups milk	3 egg yolks

1. Dissolve ½ cup sugar in water in a saucepan over moderate heat. When it is completely dissolved, bring to a boil and continue boiling until sugar begins to brown or caramelize. Divide caramelized sugar among six individual custard dishes. Set aside.

2. Bring milk to just below a simmer in a saucepan with vanilla bean. Cover and let steep.

3. Beat remaining ½ cup sugar into eggs and yolks until light and foamy. Continue beating while adding the hot milk in a thin stream. Pour custard into carmel-lined dishes.

4. Place custard dishes on a shallow baking sheet and put into lower third of a 350° oven. Pour water onto baking sheet to come part way

up sides of dishes. Bake approximately 35 to 40 minutes. Do not overbake. Custards should not crack. They will still be slightly shaky when done. Cool and refrigerate. To serve, run a table knife around the edge of the custard and invert on individual serving plates. Enjoy.

Crème Carmel is a classic finish to a meal. Mexico, Spain, France and Italy all have crème carmels. It's a traditional dessert.

Dinner for Six

Kir au Champagne

Ikra

Asparagus Vinaigrette Salad

Salmon au Champagne

Quail in Vodka and Sour Cream

Fresh Vegetables in Season

Floating Island Meringue "Tastevin"

Coffee "Tastevin"

Wine:

With Salad—a French Vouvray, 1978
With Salmon—Domaine Chandon Brut Sparkling Wine
With Quail—Savigny-les-Beaune, Villamont, 1973
With Dessert—Ste. Michelle Ice Wine, 1978

Emile Ninaud and Jacques Boiroux, Owners
Jacques Boiroux, Head Chef

LE TASTEVIN

Since leaving France in 1964, Emile Ninaud has been a restaurant man. His experience with a retail wine shop called Champion Cellars, led him to form the Seattle Chapter of Les Amis du Vin in 1971, and the wine shop is still known as the Les Amis du Vin outlet today. In 1976 China-born Emile and Jacques Boiroux, originally of Le Mans in Normandy, France, decided to open a wine-oriented restaurant. In those days the burgeoning Northwest wine industry was getting started, the wine spectrum was enlarging, and there was a great need for a good restaurant featuring quality wines at reasonable prices.

The owners chose Le Tastevin, meaning "the wine tasting cup," as the establishment's name, and the restaurant took off to such an extent that they were soon persuaded to move from their charming 80 seat location to the present 225 capacity restaurant. A big jump, but the transition was smooth and the quality remained constant, and in some respects, better. Now ideally situated only a few blocks from the Seattle Center, Le Tastevin derives the greater part of its clientele from the art and entertainment centers nearby. Be they opera, symphony, theater or Supersonics fans, such guests can be found mingling at Le Tastevin.

Seattle being the capital of the world for fresh salmon, Dungeness crab, Olympia oysters and Penn Cove mussels, Le Tastevin is the ideal place to come for seafood delights such as the Kulibiac of Salmon served with a butter and lime sauce, or the Moules Marinières cooked in a broth of Sauvignon Blanc. The Beef Wellington with Béarnaise is a favorite and can be complimented by "one of the best wine lists in the country." Extensive and carefully planned to reflect a welcome array of quality and prices, this wine list has been widely acclaimed and has earned the restaurant several prestigious awards of excellence.

Le Tastevin has always been a trendsetter in the preparation of innovative dishes. The owners bypass nouvelle cuisine, yet the food is served in a very healthy, imaginative way. The portions are large, carefully prepared with a light use of spices, and startlingly attractive. Most of all, the consistency is great. Emile and Jacques feel certain that "people return because of the assurance of not being disappointed."

From frequent wine tastings which support its name, to regular afternoon buffet hours, to marvelous evening meals, Le Tastevin truly stands for consistency and high quality. Owners Emile and Jacques, being "true food and wine lovers" themselves, couldn't possibly settle for anything else.

19 West Harrison

KIR AU CHAMPAGNE

Crème de cassis
Champagne

Per drink: Pour ½ teaspoon crème de cassis in each wine glass. Top with a dry champagne.

Kir is a favorite apéritif in Burgundy; it can be made with a still dry white wine.

IKRA
Poor Man's Caviar

2 *large eggplants*	*Salt*
1 *ounce olive oil*	*Pepper*
3 *shallots, minced*	1 *ounce red wine vinegar*
1 *teaspoon tomato paste*	*Melba toast*

1. Bake the eggplants whole at 375° for 1 hour until soft. Remove the meat of the eggplants and finely chop.
2. Heat olive oil in a pan and sauté minced shallots until golden. Add the eggplant and tomato paste. Salt and pepper to taste and add vinegar.
3. Cook for 5 to 10 minutes on simmer. Chill overnight. Serve in a bowl with melba toast.

ASPARAGUS VINAIGRETTE SALAD

1½ *pounds fresh asparagus*	1 *lemon, cut into 6 wedges*
6 *leaves Bibb lettuce*	6 *anchovy filets*
6 *slices tomato*	6 *sprigs parsley*
6 *large black olives*	*Oil and vinegar dressing*

1. Blanch the asparagus in boiling salted water until tender. Cool

quickly and divide between six chilled salad plates, placing on top of a Bibb leaf.

2. Garnish with slices of tomato, olives, lemon wedges, anchovies and parsley. Top everything with your favorite oil and vinegar dressing.

To keep asparagus very green, add a pinch of baking soda to the boiling water. The best season for asparagus is from March to May.

Le Tastevin prefers to have, as in France, an appetizer before the meal and a small, simple salad following, but since Americans are used to eating a rather large salad before dinner, we comply with the American tradition unless requested otherwise.

SALMON AU CHAMPAGNE

6 *7-ounce salmon filets*	*Pepper*
1½ *sticks butter*	1 *bottle (tenth) Christian*
3 *shallots, minced*	*Brothers Chablis*
8 *mushroom caps, fluted*	½ *cup flour*
Salt	1 *cup heavy cream, whipped*

1. Butter the bottom of a 3 inch deep skillet. Sprinkle the shallots on the butter and then place the salmon filets on top of shallots. Arrange the mushroom caps around filets. Salt and pepper the fish. Cover with the Chablis. Poach for 15 to 20 minutes.

2. Meanwhile, make a beurre manié with one stick of softened butter by adding ½ cup of flour and thoroughly mixing together. This will be the thickening agent for the sauce. Do not cook the flour and butter; it is not a roux.

3. Remove the salmon filets to a warm platter, placing a mushroom cap on each filet. Bring the stock in which you have cooked the fish to a boil and add the beurre manié a little at a time until the sauce is thick enough to use a whip to stir.

4. Simmer for 5 minutes and add 2 tablespoons of softened butter in small pieces. Mix the whipped cream into the sauce and season to

taste. Strain sauce through fine mesh strainer and pour over the fish. Glaze the sauce under the broiler until golden brown.

Fresh steelhead or fresh trout could be used instead of the salmon.

Our fish is always fresh—this is no problem. We even have fresh scallops from the East coast; they are a house specialty.

QUAIL IN VODKA AND SOUR CREAM

12 quail	2 ounces vodka
Salt	5 medium shallots, chopped
Pepper	1 glass of Chablis
Oregano	(6 to 8 ounces)
Basil	3 ounces brown stock
2 cloves garlic	2 pints sour cream
½ pound butter	Watercress

1. Season the quail with salt, pepper, oregano, basil and garlic. In a cocotte (deep cooking skillet), brown them in the butter and flambé with 1 ounce of vodka. Cover the cocotte and simmer for 5 to 10 minutes.

2. Remove the birds to a warm platter. Sauté the chopped shallots in a roasting pan until they are golden brown. Deglaze with the Chablis and reduce the sauce to one-half (by boiling over moderately high heat.

3. Add the brown stock and cook for 5 to 10 minutes. Blend in the sour cream and cook very slowly. (If the sauce seems to need thickening, use some cornstarch.)

4. Add the quail to the sauce and simmer for 5 to 10 minutes more. Season to taste. Arrange the birds on a serving platter. Cover them with some of the sauce to which you have added a good shot of vodka. Serve the remaining sauce in a sauce boat. Garnish the platter with watercress.

   Squabs, pheasant, partridge or doves (closest to quail) can be used. Gin may be substituted for vodka for more flavor.

   We are a good, typical French restaurant of the provinces.

FRESH VEGETABLES IN SEASON

For example:

1 to 1½ pounds fresh green beans

1. Wash and remove ends and string, if any. Cut lengthwise on the diagonal into thin strips.
2. In small amount of boiling water, cook uncovered 5 minutes, and then covered for 5 to 15 minutes.

Fresh green beans are in season all year round.

Fresh ingredients are more available here than in France. For example, we can get many more fresh vegetables all year round. It takes a little shopping around, but it is easy to find anything. You must be on good terms with your suppliers (paying bills on time, etc.) and they will always help you out.

FLOATING ISLAND MERINGUE "TASTEVIN"

1 *quart milk*	½ *tablespoon cornstarch*
6 *eggs, separated*	½ *teaspoon vanilla*
½ *pound sugar*	1 *ounce Cointreau liqueur*

1. Bring milk to a simmer. While you are whipping egg whites into stiff peaks, add ¼ pound of sugar slowly. Divide the meringue into six egg shapes and poach in simmering milk for about 30 seconds on each side.
2. With a slotted spoon, scoop the meringues out of the milk and arrange on a serving platter.
3. To make the custard cream, whip the egg yolk and ¼ pound sugar together till it forms a ribbon on your spoon. Add the cornstarch and mix well. Add vanilla and the hot milk left over from the poaching.

Cook the mixture until it thickens, without boiling. (Boiling will make it curdle). Flavor with the Cointreau and strain over the poached meringue. Refrigerate.

4. When serving, you can decorate the dessert with mint leaves, candied violets, or anything of your choice.

Americans are used to eating much heavier desserts than the French. We serve delicious chocolate mousse and cheesecake, but personally we prefer the traditional fresh fruit or sherbet, or something a bit lighter such as this Floating Island Meringue.

COFFEE "TASTEVIN"

Per 12-ounce glass:

½ shot Cointreau	*Strong black coffee*
½ shot Kahlua	*Whipped cream*
1 shot dark crème de cacao	

Heat glasses. Add liqueurs and fill with coffee. Top with whipped cream.

1**3** COINS

Dinner for Four

Steak Tartare

Spinach Salad, 13 Coins

Veal Scaloppine alla Marsala

Zabaglione

Beverages:

With Steak Tartare—Veedercrest Chardonnay, 1978

With Spinach Salad—sparkling mineral water

With Veal Scaloppine—Clos du Bois Reserve Cabernet Sauvignon, 1974

With Zabaglione—Grand Marnier

John C. and Donna Vertrees, William J. and Jeanne P. Boyce,
and Fred S. and Julie Jones, Owners

Mike Eberlein, Executive Chef

THIRTEEN COINS

In 1967, James D. Ward took the name for his new restaurant from an old South American legend about a poor cowboy and a rich and beautiful rancher's daughter. When the cowboy asked the girl's father for her hand in marriage, the man asked what the boy had to offer. "Sir, I love your daughter with all my heart, but all I have to give are these thirteen coins. The father was so touched by the boy's honesty and sincerity that he gave his blessings and a fine dowry to the happy couple. The thirteen coins have become symbolic of everlasting good wishes.

In addition to the good wishes, the 13 Coins Restaurants offer a unique approach to dining in their innovative, never-closing eateries with an over 130-item menu. According to co-owner Jeanne Boyce, "We have as many items in the front lines for our chefs to use as most places have in their entire stock." Because they serve everything on the menu 24 hours a day, the 13 Coins has been called "a restaurant that can't tell time."

"We have a very steady crew here, and it is the customers who ultimately reap the benefits of this, for we all get to know our guests quite well. The waiters are mostly all full time and have been with us for years—they consider it a profession. Our cooks, too, think of themselves as professionals, and it shows."

Exhibition cooking is a big attraction at the 13 Coins. Cooks have been known to flame orders, dance around to music and open and shut oven doors using their feet with such dramatic energy that one of them has coined the phrase "break cooking" to describe their antics. The extravagant show and pleasing wood and leather decor of the 13 Coins have since been copied by many, but rarely with the same success.

The owners feel that the 13 Coins is so successful because it is so adaptable. "The Coins can be anything you want it to be. It is Eggs Benedict for breakfast. It is business lunch. It is afternoon ham and eggs. It is an elegant dinner house. It is jeans after the softball game. It is tails after the opera. The 13 Coins welcomes everyone."

125 Boren Avenue North

18000 Pacific Highway South

STEAK TARTARE

6 ounces tenderloin steak	Salt and pepper
2 egg yolks	2 tablespoons finely
1 teaspoon Cognac	chopped onion
⅛ teaspoon dry mustard	2 tablespoons capers,
Dash Worcestershire	non-peri (a Spanish
sauce	caper)

1. Trim tenderloin so that there is no fat or gristle. Chop very fine or coarsely grind.
2. Add 1 egg yolk, Cognac, dry mustard, Worcestershire sauce, salt and pepper to taste. Mix very well.
3. Form a patty on a plate, then garnish with chopped onions and capers. Place other egg yolk in the center of the patty.
4. Serve with melba toast or an assortment of crackers.

SPINACH SALAD, 13 COINS

2 to 3 bunches fresh SPINACH	6 pieces bacon, cooked and
DRESSING	chopped
4 hard-cooked eggs, whites	
only, shredded	

1. Wash spinach three or four times. Drain well. Pick leaves with least amount of stem and place in salad bowl and lightly toss with Dressing.
2. Sprinkle with shredded egg whites and bacon bits.

SPINACH SALAD DRESSING

3 egg yolks
1 cup oil
1 teaspoon lemon juice
1 tablespoon ground capers
1½ teaspoons dry mustard
1½ teaspoons black pepper

2 teaspoons granulated
garlic
2 teaspoons salt
¼ cup sugar
¼ cup catsup
1 cup red wine vinegar

1. Whip egg yolks until fluffy.
2. Beating continuously, slowly add half the oil to egg yolks, then slowly add all other ingredients except catsup and vinegar.
3. While continuing to beat vigorously, slowly add the remaining oil, then catsup and vinegar.

This dressing should have the consistency of thin mayonnaise. The taste should be a light sweet and sour, the color slightly pink. The dressing may be kept refrigerated for up to two weeks.

VEAL SCALOPPINE ALLA MARSALA

24 ounces veal, cut into
12 pieces and pounded
Salt and pepper
⅓ cup flour
1 cube whole butter

12 ounces sliced mushrooms
⅔ of a lemon
½ cup sauterne
½ cup Marsala wine

1. Season the veal with salt and pepper and flour lightly. Sauté over high heat in butter 3 or 4 minutes on each side.
2. Add the mushrooms and sauté.
3. Squeeze the lemon over the mushrooms and veal and add the sauterne and the Marsala. Cook quickly until the sauce forms a

semi-thick consistency. Serve with buttered noodles, rice or potatoes.

If a gas stove is used, allow the wine to ignite.

ZABAGLIONE

1 *cup sugar*	12 *egg yolks*
1 *cup straight sherry*	

In a double boiler on high heat, place all ingredients at once and proceed to use electric mixer on high to beat all ingredients until a light and airy pudding texture is achieved. Serve immediately while hot.

TRADER VIC'S

Dinner for Six

Crab Rangoon

Tofu Pâté

Panko Beef

Sunflower Seed Salad

Mahi-Mahi Tofu Dumplings

Barbecued Pork Loin, Luau Style

Asparagus Chinese Style

Pake Noodles

Coconut Mousse

Wine:

Ste. Michelle Johannisberg Riesling, 1976
Callaway Chenin Blanc, 1977
Louis Martini Zinfandel, 1976

Harry Wong, General Manager
York Choy, Head Chef

TRADER VIC'S

Harry Wong has managed the Trader Vic's in Seattle for the past 30 years. During this time he has seen the original bar, which opened as the Outrigger in 1948, expanded to include a restaurant in 1954, and the changing of the name to Trader Vic's in 1960. The name, of course, refers to Victor Bergeron, who opened the first Trader Vic's in Oakland in 1934. Currently there are 20 restaurants comprising this unique chain.

Trader Vic's decor follows an attractive South Seas theme throughout, and is set off by the authentic Chinese ovens which are in full view for the guests through a glass room. "An interesting feature of these ovens," explains Harry, "is the suspension of the meat inside, providing indirect heat and preventing the meat from drying out."

Another special attraction at Trader Vic's is the complete private dining room and bar, which can accommodate over 50 people. Trader Vic's boasts one of the most tightly run and efficiently operated kitchens in town. Head chef York Choy and his staff oversee the preparation of over 140 items on the menu, from fresh seafood and continental dishes to Polynesian delights. Their Indonesian lamb roast is perhaps the oldest favorite offered, as it "has always been very popular since day one. Nobody else makes it quite like we do."

Quality is the byword at all Trader Vic's restaurants. Everything is fresh and the objective is to give the customers their money's worth. Most recently Trader Vic's has streamlined their menu so that it is now easier to read and select from, thus further looking after the interests of their guests. With a climate like that found in Seattle, what could be better than escaping to Trader Vic's to sip an exotic drink and to dream of sunny skies, white sand beaches, palm trees and tropical moonlight.

Westin Hotel
1900 5th Avenue

CRAB RANGOON

¼ pound crab meat
¼ pound cream cheese
Dash A-1 sauce
Dash garlic powder
Salt and pepper

2 pounds Won Ton noodle
squares
1 egg yolk, beaten
Cooking oil

1. Chop crab and blend with cream cheese and A-1 sauce. Add garlic powder, salt and pepper; blend thoroughly in a mixing bowl.
2. Put ½ teaspoon of the mixture in center of noodle square. Fold square over, diagonally. Moisten the edges slightly with the beaten egg yolk and twist together. Corners may be folded in.
3. Fry in deep hot fat until delicately browned. Serve hot. Catsup or hot mustard may be used as dips.

This may take up to 60 pieces, depending on how much of the mixture is placed in the noodle. The extras may be frozen for future use.

The Won Ton noodle squares, or Won Ton wrappers, can be found in the frozen food section in many grocery stores.

TOFU PÂTÉ

½ pound uncooked chicken
livers
1 teaspoon chopped shallots
Pinch salt
Pinch mace
Pinch nutmeg
Pinch sage
Clarified butter
1 ounce brandy
2 ounces tofu (firm)

1 ounce Havarti cheese (or a
smooth Swiss cheese)
1 ounce cream cheese
1 ounce whipping cream
2 tablespoons unflavored
gelatin
5 to 6 ounces chicken or beef
consommé
1 hard-cooked egg, diced
¼ cup pistachio nuts

1. Sauté the livers, shallots and four spices in clarified butter until the

is cooked medium rare to medium. Add the brandy and flame. Place the livers, tofu, cheeses and cream in a food processor or blender. Add 1 tablespoon unflavored gelatin which has been dissolved in ½ ounce consommé. Blend until very smooth in texture.

2. In the bottom of a pâté mold, pour half of the consommé mixture consisting of 4 ounces consommé and 1 tablespoon unflavored gelatin. Add the diced egg. Chill until stiff. Then add the pâté mixture.

3. Cover the entire pâté with ⅛ inch more consommé and ¼ cup pistachio nuts. Chill and serve with crackers, such as buttered rye.

This will yield one pound of pâté. However, do not freeze leftovers, or the pâté will lose its composition. Pâte can be made days in advance.

Almonds, macadamia nuts or peanuts can be used instead of pistachios.

PANKO BEEF

2½ to 3 *ounces flank steak*	1 *cup BATTER*
Salt	½ *cup Japanese bread*
¼ *teaspoon teriyaki sauce*	*crumbs (Panko brand)*
Few shreds fresh ginger	*Cooking oil*

1. Trim all fat from flank steak and cut across the grain into ½-inch slices; cut each piece into 2-inch lengths. Salt the steak strips and pour over them the teriyaki sauce mixed with the fresh ginger. Dip the meat into the batter, then coat thoroughly with Japanese bread crumbs.

2. Fry in deep hot oil to a golden brown. Serve with hot mustard.

Panko Japanese bread crumbs are made from rice. They can be obtained at Japanese grocery stores. If this ingredient is not available, nothing can be substituted to produce even near the same results.

BATTER

4 tablespoons flour
1 tablespoon cornstarch
½ cup water

1 egg
½ teaspoon baking powder
1 teaspoon oil

Put all ingredients in blender until smooth.

SUNFLOWER SEED SALAD

2 cups fresh bean sprouts
¼ cup shelled raw sunflower
    seeds
¼ cup julienned cooked
    white chicken meat
⅓ cup julienned barbecued
    pork
¼ medium jalapeño
    pepper, very thinly
    sliced
3 whole green onions,
    julienned

½ tablespoon red wine
    vinegar
⅓ cup safflower oil
    Juice of ½ lemon
½ teaspoon Dijon mustard
    Salt and pepper to taste
1 head iceberg lettuce
1 tomato, cut in wedges
3 hard-cooked eggs, cut in
    half
12 to 18 black olives
    Water cress or peppercress

1. Blanch the bean sprouts in boiling water 1½ to 2 minutes. Drain and cool. Simmer sunflower seeds for 10 minutes in water. Drain and cool.

2. Place chicken, pork, jalapeño pepper and onions in a bowl. Add bean sprouts.

3. Mix together vinegar, oil, lemon juice and mustard. Combine with meat and sprout mixture, mixing well. Salt and pepper to taste.

4. Form a lettuce cap for each person on a salad plate. Using a cup, mound salad mixture on each plate. Sprinkle sunflower seeds over each salad. Decorate with tomato wedges, eggs, black olives and cress.

All the cutting can be done ahead of time. This is a good luncheon salad also. Bay shrimp can be substituted for chicken and pork.

MAHI-MAHI TOFU DUMPLINGS

3 *pounds Mahi-Mahi*
3 *tablespoons fresh shallots*
6 *egg whites*
1 *quart whipping cream*
  Salt, pepper, Aromat
  seasoning
  Dash Worcestershire
  sauce

SAUCE
2 *tablespoons Hollandaise*
2 *tablespoons whole cream*
4 *cakes tofu, diced in ¼"*
  cubes
3 *tablespoons Bay shrimp*

1. Grind Mahi-Mahi and shallots finely. Put in a blender with egg whites and whipping cream until very smooth. Add salt, pepper, Aromat seasoning and dash of Worcestershire sauce. Mix thoroughly.

2. Using 2 tablespoons each of the mixture, shape into quenelles (dumplings). Poach in salted water until firm. Keep warm.

3. Using 1½ cups of Sauce, fold in Hollandaise and whole cream. Add the heated quenelles, tofu and Bay shrimp. If too thick, add some chicken stock.

SAUCE

3 *bottles (7 ounces each)*
  clam juice
1 *ounce lemon juice*
2 *ounces dry white wine*
1 *tablespoon Aromat*
  seasoning

½ *tablespoon salt*
¼ *teaspoon white pepper*
1 *quart water*
4 *tablespoons light roux*

Place all ingredients except roux in a saucepan and bring to a boil.

Add the roux and cook to medium thickness. Simmer for 5 to 10 minutes. Keep warm.

When making this dish, be sure to heat the sauce separately from the quenelles and tofu.

You could also use filet of sole or red snapper.

BARBECUED PORK LOIN, LUAU STYLE

1 *cup soy sauce*
1 *tablespoon sugar*
½ *cup canned crushed pineapple*
1½ *ounces unsweetened pineapple juice*

1 *clove garlic, crushed*
1 *small piece fresh ginger, grated (the size of 2 cloves of garlic)*
6 *1" thick loin pork chops*

1. Mix marinade by combining first six ingredients and pouring into a shallow glass, enamel or stainless steel baking pan.
2. Trim meat of all fat leaving just a layer covering the lean part of the meat. Marinate the pork 4 to 6 hours.
3. Preheat oven to 350°. Place pork on rack of baking pan; bake for 20 to 30 minutes.

You should never use aluminum cooking utensils when using soy sauce.

ASPARAGUS CHINESE STYLE

1 tablespoon cubed lean
  pork
1 teaspoon peanut oil
1 pound fresh asparagus,
  cut into 2" pieces

1 cup chicken stock
  Cornstarch and water
  mixture

1. Sauté the pork in peanut oil. When browned on all sides add asparagus and chicken stock. Cook until boiling.
2. Thicken sauce with the cornstarch and water mixture; stir over low heat until desired consistency.

This could be made with any vegetable in season.

PAKE NOODLES

2 cups cooked fresh egg
  noodles
3 tablespoons butter

2 tablespoons bread crumbs
2 tablespoons sesame seeds
  Salt and pepper

Mix the heated noodles with butter, bread crumbs and sesame seeds. Salt and pepper to taste.

COCONUT MOUSSE

1½ pints half and half	Pinch salt
½ bottle Trader Vic's Koko Kreme Syrup	1 teaspoon sugar
1 tablespoon unflavored gelatin	½ pound pound-cake
4 eggs, separated	4 ounces coconut milk
	Pistachio nuts

1. Mix together half and half, Koko Kreme, gelatin, egg yolks and salt in top of double boiler.
2. Cook over medium heat, stirring constantly, just until ingredients are dissolved. Put into a bowl with an ice bed underneath. Chill until thick.
3. Whip the egg whites separately till stiff. Add the sugar to the whites.
4. Fold egg whites into batter. Pour mixture into 4-ounce molds.
5. Cut pound cake ¼ inch thick into the size of the bottom of the molds. Place pound cake on batter and chill until firm.
6. Unmold and place on serving dish. Whip the coconut milk and pour over top. Sprinkle with pistachio nuts.

RECIPE INDEX

Appetizers

Beverages

Desserts and Dessert Accents

RECIPE INDEX

RECIPE INDEX

RECIPE INDEX

NOTES

DINING IN-WITH THE GREAT CHEFS
A Collection of Gourmet Recipes from the Finest Chefs in the Country

Each book contains gourmet recipes for complete meals from the chefs of 21 great restaurants.

___ *Dining In–Baltimore* $7.95	___ *Dining In–Monterey Peninsula* 7.95
___ *Dining In–Boston (Revised)* 8.95	___ *Dining In–Napa Valley* 8.95
___ *Dining In–Chicago, Vol. III* 8.95	___ *Dining In–New Orleans* 8.95
___ *Dining In–Cleveland* 8.95	___ *Dining In–Philadelphia* 8.95
___ *Dining In–Dallas (Revised)* 8.95	___ *Dining In–Phoenix* 8.95
___ *Dining In–Denver* 7.95	___ *Dining In–Pittsburgh (Revised)* 7.95
___ *Dining In–Hampton Roads* 8.95	___ *Dining In–Portland* 7.95
___ *Dining In–Hawaii* 7.95	___ *Dining In–St. Louis* 7.95
___ *Dining In–Houston, Vol. II* 7.95	___ *Dining In–Salt Lake City* 8.95
___ *Dining In–Kansas City (Revised)* 7.95	___ *Dining In–San Francisco, Vol II* 7.95
___ *Dining In–Los Angeles (Revised)* 8.95	___ *Dining In–Seattle* 8.95
___ *Dining In–Manhattan* 8.95	___ *Dining In–Sun Valley* 7.95
___ *Dining In–Miami* 8.95	___ *Dining In–Toronto* 7.95
___ *Dining In–Milwaukee* 7.95	___ *Dining In–Vancouver, B.C.* 8.95
___ *Dining In–Minneapolis/St. Paul, Vol. II* . . $8.95	___ *Dining In–Washington, D.C.* 8.95

☐ Check (✔) here if you would like to have a different Dining In–Cookbook sent to you once a month. Payable by MasterCard or VISA. Returnable if not satisfied.

☐ Payment enclosed $_____ (Please include $1.00 postage and handling for each book)

☐ Charge to:

Visa # _____ Exp. Date _____

MasterCard # _____ Exp. Date _____

Signature _____

Name _____

Address _____

City _____ State ____ Zip _____

SHIP TO (if other than name and address above):

Name _____

Address _____

City _____ State ____ Zip _____

PEANUT BUTTER PUBLISHING
911 Western Avenue, Suite 401, Maritime Building ▪ Seattle, WA 98104 ▪ (206) 628-6200

SGCF1085